Praise for *Start With What W...*

'Rather than waiting for a magic bullet starting today. Andy helps you see the resources and talents you have already, but just haven't got around to using properly or fully enough. Even better, the process creates engagement and excitement among employees, because the process honours their expertise and abilities.'

Rooney Anand, former CEO of Greene King Plc; Senior Independent Director, Morrisons plc

'Leaders don't always realise how much untapped potential, strength and opportunity their organisation has. We've had great results from starting with what was already working. Andy's book will get you to see your business in a new light so that you can do that too.'

Matthew Crummack, Group CEO, GoCo Group plc (GoCompare)

'The world needs inspired leaders who excel at finding and releasing potential. Andy's book Start With What Works is a gamechanger for those who want to accelerate their business growth with greater inspiration and less risk and frustration.'

Nancy MacKay, CEO and Founder, MacKay CEO Forums

'Clear, actionable advice for any organisation seeking to grow or innovate. Before you start throwing money at the problem, unlock your hidden potential.'

Michael Smets, Professor of Management, Saïd Business School, University of Oxford

Start With What Works

Pearson

At Pearson, we have a simple mission: to help people make more of their lives through learning.

We combine innovative learning technology with trusted content and educational expertise to provide engaging and effective learning experiences that serve people wherever and whenever they are learning.

From classroom to boardroom, our curriculum materials, digital learning tools and testing programmes help to educate millions of people worldwide – more than any other private enterprise.

Every day our work helps learning flourish, and wherever learning flourishes, so do people.

To learn more, please visit us at **www.pearson.com/uk**

Start With What Works

A faster way to grow your business

Andy Bass, PhD

Pearson

Harlow, England • London • New York • Boston • San Francisco • Toronto • Sydney
Dubai • Singapore • Hong Kong • Tokyo • Seoul • Taipei • New Delhi
Cape Town • São Paulo • Mexico City • Madrid • Amsterdam • Munich • Paris • Milan

PEARSON EDUCATION LIMITED
KAO Two
KAO Park
Harlow CM17 9NA
United Kingdom
Tel: +44 (0)1279 623623
Web: www.pearson.com/uk

First edition published 2021 (print and electronic)

© Pearson Education Limited 2021 (print and electronic)

The right of Andy Bass to be identified as author of this work has been asserted by him in accordance with the Copyright, Designs and Patents Act 1988.

The print publication is protected by copyright. Prior to any prohibited reproduction, storage in a retrieval system, distribution or transmission in any form or by any means, electronic, mechanical, recording or otherwise, permission should be obtained from the publisher or, where applicable, a licence permitting restricted copying in the United Kingdom should be obtained from the Copyright Licensing Agency Ltd, Barnard's Inn, 86 Fetter Lane, London EC4A 1EN.

The ePublication is protected by copyright and must not be copied, reproduced, transferred, distributed, leased, licensed or publicly performed or used in any way except as specifically permitted in writing by the publishers, as allowed under the terms and conditions under which it was purchased, or as strictly permitted by applicable copyright law. Any unauthorised distribution or use of this text may be a direct infringement of the author's and the publisher's rights and those responsible may be liable in law accordingly.

All trademarks used herein are the property of their respective owners. The use of any trademark in this text does not vest in the author or publisher any trademark ownership rights in such trademarks, nor does the use of such trademarks imply any affiliation with or endorsement of this book by such owners.

Pearson Education is not responsible for the content of third-party internet sites.

ISBN: 978-1-292-34111-8 (print)
       978-1-292-34543-7 (PDF)
       978-1-292-34110-1 (ePub)

British Library Cataloguing-in-Publication Data
A catalogue record for the print edition is available from the British Library

Library of Congress Cataloging-in-Publication Data
A catalog record for the print edition is available from the Library of Congress
10 9 8 7 6 5 4 3 2 1
25 24 23 22 21

Cover design by Rogue Four Design

Print edition typeset in 10/14 pt Charter ITC Pro by SPi Global
Printed by Ashford Colour Press Ltd, Gosport

NOTE THAT ANY PAGE CROSS REFERENCES REFER TO THE PRINT EDITION

To Barbara

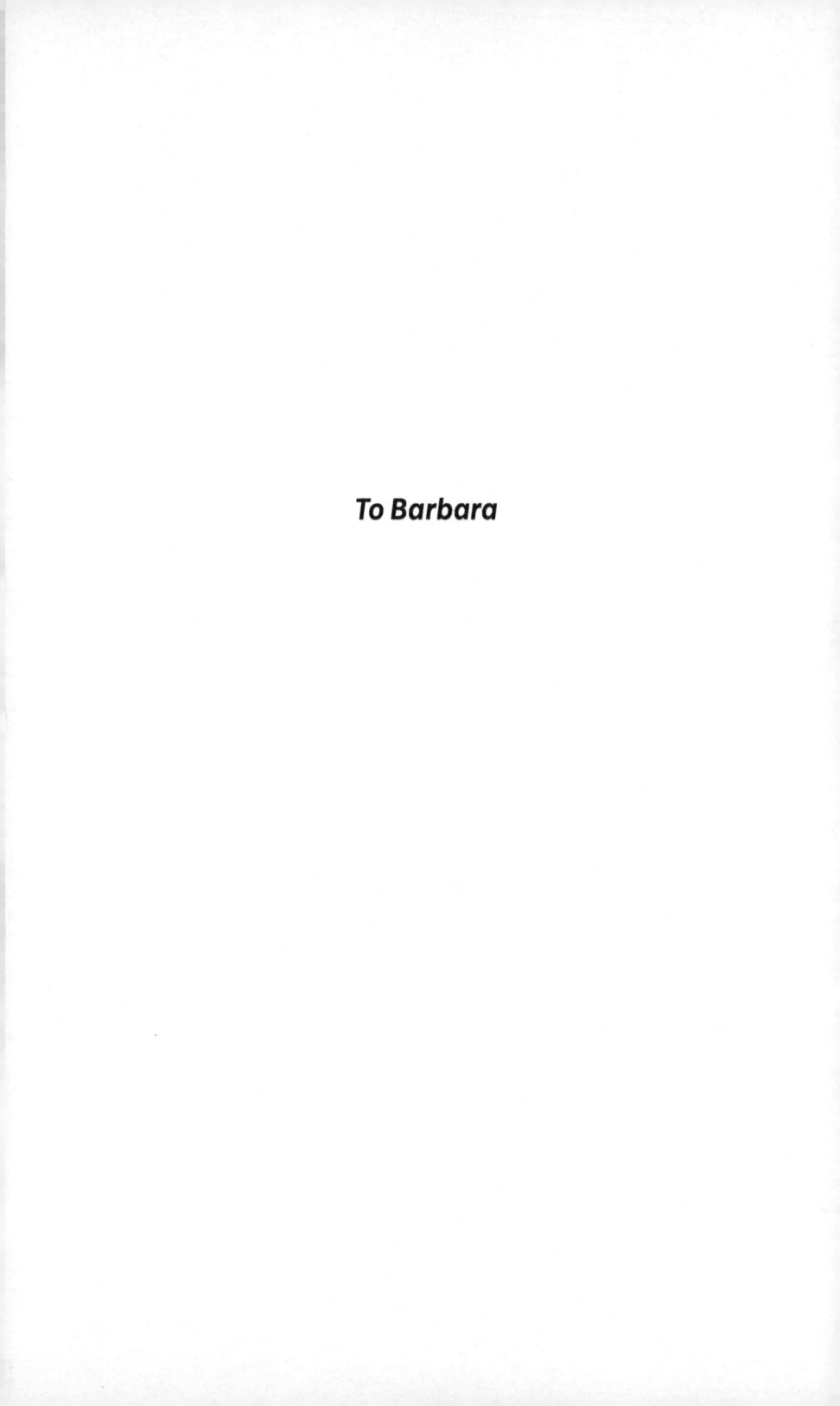

Contents

Foreword by Rory Sutherland — xi
Preface — xv
Introduction — xvii

1. Why Start with What Works? — 1
2. How We Miss Hidden Potential — 19
3. Principle One: Recombine Existing Elements So They Create More Value — 33
4. Principle Two: Escape from Fixed Purposes — 53
5. Principle Three: Reverse Engineer Yourself — 73
6. Principle Four: Let the World Teach You — 93
7. Principle Five: Watch What Actually Happens — 109
8. Principle Six: Find the Few Things That Really Make a Difference — 125
9. Principle Seven: Use *Very* Plain Words to Describe What You Want — 145
10. Principle Eight: Look Beyond 'Us and Them' — 159

11.	Principle Nine: Bring Customers Inside	177
12.	Principle Ten: Give Control to Get Control	191
13.	Getting Started, Releasing Change	207
14.	Epilogue: You Go First	227

Further Resources	241
Notes	243
Index	249
Acknowledgements	261
About the Author	263
Publisher's Acknowledgements	265

Foreword

by Rory Sutherland, Vice-Chairman, Ogilvy

In Robert Cialdini's excellent book *Pre-suasion*, which would make a fine companion read to this volume, the author makes a vital but seemingly implausible assertion about the nature of human attention: rather than paying attention to things which are important, the human brain is prone to operate in reverse: it deems most important those things to which we devote the most attention.

Therein, I think, lies a central problem of business decision-making: one which this book will do a great deal to help you correct. Because this book corrects this attention bias by providing you with a range of entirely new standpoints from which to observe a business. From these new perspectives emerge a whole range of new and original possibilities for growth and worthwhile innovation.

The title of the book seems like common sense. But how often have you held a meeting to discuss what is going well in your business – those good aspects which need to be amplified? Not often, I venture. Instead our focus is mostly on problems.

And especially on those problems which happen to be easily quantifiable.

As a result, a small and selective group of concerns come to dominate the horizon. It's an example of what the psychologist Daniel Kahneman calls WYSIATI or 'What you see is all there is'.

What this book does is something vitally important. It reorients its readers' views and encourages us to look at things in entirely fresh ways. From this emerge different perspectives which may be entirely complementary to those which businesses tend to prioritise.

It is an interesting reflection on business perspectives that the phrase 'What gets measured gets managed' is usually a) attributed to Peter Drucker, (who never said it) and b) quoted approvingly. Never mind that Drucker would never have said something so stupid, as anybody with a passing knowledge of his work or intellectual influences might have spotted immediately. But, more important still, the person who did indeed say it meant it as a criticism, not an exhortation.

V. F. Ridgway originated the principle in 1956 in an article entitled 'Dysfunctional Consequences of Performance Measurements'. Simon Caulkin, a columnist, condensed his argument as follows:

'What gets measured gets managed — even when it's pointless to measure and manage it, and even if it harms the purpose of the organisation to do so.'

Ridgway clearly was onto something in 1956. Not everything that matters can be measured. Not everything that we can measure matters. And, as Andy Bass would astutely add, 'What gets measured often gets gamed'.

The London Business School Professor Jules Goddard adds the observation that by obsessing about those parts of a business which happen to take numerical form, we may completely distort our view of what a business should be focusing on and trying to improve. As he puts it, the standard income statement has one revenue line, and six or seven cost lines. And we tend to pay attention to those things in precisely that ratio. This then leads to a maniacal focus on cost-cutting, as though this were somehow the only thing your customers cared about. Yet, as you'll read in the following pages, many customers, even in B2B, have a much more nuanced view of value than conventional business logic believes.

With all this obsession with quantification, it's too easy to overlook the fact that if your business has been in existence for some length of time, it's highly likely that – even if only by accident – it has acquired some number of useful insights or skills which are far more valuable than you know. These are the commercial equivalent of 'Cash in the Attic'.

Why not spend some time assessing and appreciating those things? And exploring how your best qualities might be expanded, decoupled, repurposed or rebundled? Just as it has been said that 'We shape our buildings and then our buildings shape us', the same can be said of business categories. We define business categories for reasons of convenience and ease of comparison, but then end up narrowly defined and indeed constrained by those same definitions. After a time we mistake the map for reality.

The industry in which I work, the advertising industry, has not been paid on media commission since about 1989, or not to any significant extent. Yet its muscle-memory of being remunerated this way still dominates: it behaves as though the only possible business problems which it can solve are those where the solution involves a significant amount of bought media.

This is an extraordinarily self-limiting belief, which narrows and underrates the value of applied creativity, wordsmithery, artistry and original thinking – for which there exists a much larger potential market far outside the marketing department of a few client companies. The advertising industry has been lethargic in spotting the fact that there is a far larger market for its acquired expertise than it has so far envisaged. A large advertising agency has the talent and resources of a general hospital, but it still has a sign outside the door that offers cosmetic surgery. It was only when Andy Main joined as Ogilvy's CEO this year, significantly not from another ad agency but from Deloitte Digital, that this myopic view began to be corrected.

I only wish I had read this book some years earlier. I would have felt far better vindicated in what I was trying to do ten years ago, when I first started a behavioural science practice within an advertising agency to solve the kind of problems agencies weren't historically asked to solve . . . but where in many cases could deliver more business value than a conventional communications approach. (Indeed I'm very flattered one or two pieces of our work appear in the following pages).

As with behavioural science, one of the delights of the Bass approach is that it is scaleable. It can work at the level of a multinational. But the same approach also pays if you're running a café.

Foreword

I first met the author through his enthusiasm for complexity theory, and research into complex systems. And I've increasingly come to believe that one of the hallmarks of any successful approach to complexity is that it has to be somewhat scale-independent. It has to have a kind of fractal quality, where you can apply the same principles to a pub as you can to a conglomerate. And so I leave you with one final tip when reading this book. Take each of the principles he mentions, and imagine them as applied to a small cafe or a tiny family run hotel. Sometimes it's much easier to understand the businesses we are customers of than the businesses we run.

What you'll see is that exactly the same possibilities emerge, regardless of the scale. Take the suggestion to unbundle the services you offer, for instance (Amazon did that with AWS, but then successful hotels can provide and sell far more than just accommodation). Or consider rebundling parts of your offer with something else, another of Andy's useful ideas. Just as I was finishing writing this foreword, someone came to me with a very sweet story about a poor young woman in Africa who sold hard boiled eggs to people working on the building sites. She'd discovered that when she bundled them with a tomato and herb salad, which cost almost nothing to produce, certainly far less than an egg, what she was selling was no longer just an egg, but lunch. And at that point, she was able to charge more than double the price of an egg for something that cost far less than two eggs to produce.

Never ever forget that lesson. Value resides in the mind of the customer. You won't understand it if you spend all your time in the office. You need a different perspective. This book will encourage you to get out and find one.

As the late John le Carré observed, 'A desk is a very dangerous place from which to view the world.'

Rory Sutherland
Westerham, Kent
December 2020

Preface

I started writing this book just prior to the onset of the COVID-19 crisis and completed it as the UK began relaxing its lockdown. I spent the lockdown in Sutton Coldfield, just outside the city of Birmingham, where the leaders of the first Industrial Revolution, people like Erasmus Darwin, James Watt, Matthew Boulton and other members of the celebrated Lunar Society, unleashed the greatest explosion of growth in world history.

During the lockdown period, I spent much of my time talking to clients about post-crisis growth, realising that more than ever the idea of Starting With What Works is particularly apposite as leaders seek new growth in a changed world.

An old teacher of mine used to like to point out that, 'At one time, there was no money in the world. And now there's a lot!' His point was that wealth isn't 'out there' waiting for us to grab it, nor is there some fixed pie to fight over. The source of wealth is human ingenuity and enterprise: the ingenuity to recognise how resources can be organised to produce value, and the enterprise to bring that value to meet the ever-evolving needs of other people.

Human beings pulled themselves up by their own bootstraps by recognising latent value in things they already had.

The world is certainly presenting new challenges. Business leaders looking for new growth now have a choice. They can dwell on evidence of how hard things are compared to the pre-COVID world. Or they can recognise that they have effectively unlimited resources – resources that would be incredible to the leaders of the first industrial revolution – and that some of the most valuable might be hiding in plain sight.

This book lays out a strategy for finding and using your overlooked resources to create new growth, and to meet myriad new needs in a changed world.

Andy Bass
The Royal Town of Sutton Coldfield
September 2020

Introduction

This book is about how to search your organisation for hidden gold. It's also about how to make new gold. I call this gold seeking-and-creating process, *Start with what works*. Let me explain what I mean.

By gold, I mean invaluable resources you can use to leave customers better off than when they found you.

Some of these resources are easy to spot. For example: smart people, proprietary processes and capital equipment. They're there, and you know they're there. They're not hiding.

But established businesses also have resources that they overlook. They're there without you noticing. You've missed their significance.

When you learn to see and then reconfigure these resources, you can create huge impact, often without capital investment.

Utilising hidden resources has a lot of advantages. It boosts your productivity, because you're getting more out of what you have already paid for. It also keeps you ahead of the competition, because by building on your own success rather than copying others, you naturally become more distinctive in the eyes of customers. As your productivity and distinctiveness flourish, you'll be building a platform for sustained growth.

Introduction

Why This Book Is for You

I've worked with hundreds of ambitious leaders and their teams in companies across many industries and geographies. Thinking about my initial meetings with my best clients, I noticed a pattern. While the problems they described may have looked different, really what they were all saying was, 'We're good. But given how good we are, we should be doing better.'

This issue of 'we should be doing better' shows up in a number of ways. For example, they might say:

- 'Our capabilities are excellent, but our value propositions don't stand out. I'm concerned that customers won't care who they buy from. How do we avoid looking like our competitors?'
- 'My people have talent, but I worry that they're getting complacent. 'World class' is a moving target. How do we raise standards and aspirations without demoralising people?'
- 'We're ingenious, but we tackle too wide a variety of problems. We accept work from all comers whether or not we really should. How do we avoid diluting our impact?'
- 'The organisation has the appetite for growth, but the advice we hear from management gurus feels too risky. It's exciting to hear about Big Hairy Audacious Goals and Silicon Valley moonshots, but what if we build it and they *don't* come?'

Business leaders of all sizes and types of companies face these kinds of questions constantly, and we'll meet many examples in the book.

Where Did the Idea of This Book Come from?

For the last fifteen years, I've worked as an independent advisor helping senior leaders around the world turn their strategies into action. Prior to that, I was a researcher in artificial intelligence, software engineering and human factors, and then spent several years as a business school lecturer, teaching and researching systems thinking and organisational change. I left the academic world because I wanted to see if the methods my colleagues and I were working on could produce results for real clients, outside the cloistered environment of the university. (The short answer to that question, by the way, is: 'Yes, with modifications' – rest assured you'll get the modified versions in this book, *and* with a minimum of jargon.)

As I started to immerse myself in client issues, and observed what managers were trying to do to improve performance in the 'real world,' I was puzzled. Many of these managers seemed to rely on a superficial – and, from the perspective of the world I'd come from, outdated – playbook. They often seemed tempted to bring in new resources, but were neglecting to figure out how to make what they already had more productive.

For a long time, I wondered if the explanation for my puzzlement was simply that the theories my colleagues and I had been working on were irrelevant to real business situations. After all, the managers I was seeing had risen to positions of success without them.

With further experience, I decided that wasn't it. As I worked with more executives in more situations, I found that the best ones clearly shared my outlook to some degree or another. Their bias was always to start with what was working, to make existing resources as productive as possible, and do more with what was already there, *before* seeking answers outside. And the results they obtained from this *start with what works* mindset stood out from the majority.

By showing you how to start with what you have, I'll show you a path to new growth while reducing frustration and unnecessary risk.

Chapter 1

Why Start with What Works?

Leave the Moonshots for Later: Just Getting into Orbit Can Be Transformational

Imagine for a moment that you're running a long-established car and truck manufacturer. Like leaders in many industries, your world is being up-ended by the most dramatic confluence of technological, environmental and political changes anyone can remember. And frankly, new competitors – unencumbered by legacy technologies and traditions – seem better suited to those changes.

How should you respond, for example, to self-driving vehicle projects by Silicon Valley tech companies such as Google's Waymo or Elon Musk's Tesla? There are many options you might consider. If you have the investment funds and can attract one of their Rock Star employees to run it, you might try to emulate their 'moonshot'[1] approach by developing your own autonomous vehicle. Or maybe you could fund a bunch of startups and hope that, even if they can't beat the disruptors head-on, they'll develop valuable intellectual property you can license out for use in others' self-driving cars. Or perhaps you could try and get involved in some kind of joint venture. I'm sure you can think of other options too.

But consider something Daimler has done. They've produced automated (not *autonomous*) versions of their trucks, fitted them with snow ploughs and programmed them to keep the runways at Frankfurt airport clear in the winter.

That's a pretty restricted move. Instead of trying to change the world, it deals with one idiosyncratic situation. It's certainly not something you could call a moonshot. Daimler's Mercedes Benz trucks are driverless, but not fully self-driving. They don't have all the sensors and intelligent decision-making to adapt to any road traffic situation. *But* they are out there now, and in this restricted but very useful case, they are:

- operating without drivers in the cab (so the airport, which has been spending €23M annually on snow clearing and de-icing, doesn't need a bunch of drivers sitting around on standby all winter);
- moving Daimler into services: recognising that many customers just want to get a job done, rather than to own and maintain a product;
- getting Daimler a reputation for high-uptime driverless solutions that are available now;
- learning in real-world situations, and getting their people involved in a different kind of innovation;
- opening up a new market: forty other airports with similar weather patterns are potential customers for just this solution, and there may be many other specialist applications that they can then move into in other industries.

While Google's Waymo, Tesla and the rest sink huge resources into high-profile, high-risk developments that are very hard for most companies to pull off – both financially and culturally – Daimler has done all this by reconfiguring what they already had or could incrementally develop. It's an approach that all businesses, regardless of size, can learn a lot from.

What have you got, and what else can you do with it?

We've talked about Daimler. Now let's start thinking about you. Where are the existing resources in your business that you could reconfigure to create new growth? Let's find out by having a sneak preview of ideas you'll meet in Chapters 4 and 5.

I'm going to be talking about three levels of resources: I term them generic, hidden and implied resources. I'll explain them all fully in due course, but let's have a look at implied resources – in some ways the most powerful – and see how they might work for you.

In the hunt for implied resources we look at what is already working and ask, 'What *must* be there in order for this to work, and what else can we do with it?'. This is where your truly unique assets might be lurking.

This thinking is applicable whatever size your business.

- **Large company.** Amazon Web Services (AWS) was launched when Amazon realised the internal capabilities that they had developed to run their main e-commerce website could be sold as a service to paying customers. As of 2020, AWS has grown to offer more than 200 services and controls more than a third of the cloud computing market, twice as much as its closest competitor. It has consistently been the most profitable division of Amazon and its primary profit driver.
- **Mid-sized company.** Lotus Cars has developed notable expertise in vehicle dynamics through its long involvement in motorsport and high-performance car manufacture. It capitalises on that know-how through its consulting arm Lotus Engineering, which consults on vehicle dynamics, suspension design and advanced propulsion systems for clients such as Tesla and Formula 1 competitors.

- **Smaller company.** Specialist software house IO Studios wanted an easy way to track its sales pipeline. The company was signed up to a well-known customer relationship management (CRM) system. The problem was that nobody liked using it, so they didn't. The company decided to use their coding skills to develop a CRM for themselves – one that they would actually like using. One day a client saw it and, impressed, asked if they could adopt it too. After other clients showed an interest, IO Studios built and launched a commercial version called Salesradar with customers ranging from freelancers to giants like Costco.

IO Studios used the same strategy as Amazon and Lotus. When they noticed that others shared a problem they had solved for themselves, they acted entrepreneurially, packaging up their solution into an attractive commercial version to seize the opportunity.

Could you do the same? Here are some questions for you to consider.

- Where have you developed solutions for your own problems that, like Amazon and IO Studios, you could package and sell to others facing similar challenges?
- What internal processes are you so good at that, like GoCompare, who provide cost-comparison software for other financial services businesses, and Ocado, who provide grocery retail technology for other supermarkets, you could offer to other people, too?
- What have you learned in the course of business that, like Lotus Cars, you could advise on or even teach others?

There's plenty more to say about all three levels of resources, and we'll cover these in the following chapters.

Starting with what works can make you a formidable competitor

The ideal business strategy is so hard to copy that you can tell your competitors all about it, and they still won't be able to copy you. Think of some of the most written-about companies in the world, like IKEA, Southwest Airlines and Apple. They are the subject of voluminous case studies. Every business school student studies them. Many people have tried to copy them, yet they continue to thrive. They are hard to copy not because their strategies are secret, but because they have developed their own unique ways of doing things. So while their competitors might know all about *what* they're doing, they can't really copy it because they can't figure out exactly *how*. Finding and building on the hidden resources you've developed in the course of business is a great defence against reverse engineering, because it makes you hard to copy.

A shift in mindset

We're going to look at how to create new growth opportunities – and lead the organisational change necessary to realise those opportunities – using the resources you already have at hand. That is, you'll learn to call upon your existing people, customers, relationships, intellectual property and know-how before making expensive and potentially risky investments in external solutions.

It sounds simple – like what most organisations are surely doing already – but very often it's not. Frequently, managers discount the value of their familiar resources, and instead, they look outside for something new.

Why do leaders discount the value of familiar resources? After all, when they acquired them, they will have had to have made a convincing investment case. They must have thought they were pretty good at the time. There are a number of reasons why perceptions of existing resources degrade over time.

- There's a strong connection in most cultures between the idea of 'new' and 'better' – and conversely of 'old' with 'not as good.' The latest iPhone or Samsung Galaxy is supposed to be the best one yet, isn't it?
- We can't help categorising. If you've always thought of your business as an engineered *products* company, for example, it can be hard to imagine your existing 'product people' providing new

value-added *services* that you realise will better meet your customers' emerging needs.
- It's not easy to be 'a prophet in your own land'. Many long-standing employees have seen their contributions discounted in favour of those of a new hire, even when the newcomer simply tells the boss something the employee has been saying for years.
- When it all looks too complicated, there's an undeniable appeal to starting again with a blank sheet of paper.

So there's a bias towards new resources. But discounting existing resources in favour of new ones can be both demoralising for incumbents and very wasteful. I've found that rather than bringing in fresh resources, it's often a lot quicker, cheaper and safer to help leaders see existing resources with fresh eyes. This book shows you how to recognise overlooked potential in existing resources, and how to flip the right switches to activate that potential.

Box 1.1
Is a new signing the answer to all of a team's prayers?

I was recently discussing these ideas with Paul Faulkner, the former CEO of the storied English football teams Aston Villa and Nottingham Forest.

As I talked to him about the bias towards new resources, Paul started to laugh.

'This is exactly what it was like running a football team,' he explained.

'I lost count of the number of times the coaches would ask me for: 'Just one more player.' I'd reply to them that there was little point buying even the best striker in the world if the team couldn't gain and keep possession of the ball and then supply it

> to that striker. I'd urge the coaching staff to work on rethinking what we did with the existing squad. I figured that then, if we did buy an expensive new player, we'd be better able to use them. And maybe we'd find that the players we already had – including last year's star signing that the coaches now seemed to be less enthusiastic about – could really flourish and bring us the results anyway.'

Starting with what works lowers your risks

Paul Faulkner (see Box 1.1) wanted his team's football coaches to do more with the existing players. It wasn't just about money. It's also about risk. Here are some of the concerns I hear from leaders seeking advice about growth.

- I'm concerned that, if I bring people in from the outside, my own people will be sceptical, or even resentful.
- I'm scared that if I bring in someone who doesn't understand what makes our business distinctive, instead of helping us, they'll inadvertently damage us.
- I might consider spending more money if I knew it would work, but what if it doesn't?
- I'm worried if we try to change and go the wrong way, that having brought in loads of expensive resources, it's going to be hard to stop the train.
- It would be better for this to be less visible until I'm happy it's going to work.
- If I bring in expensive high-profile solutions and it goes badly I'll look like an idiot.
- I don't want to commit to a methodology that might not work.
- If I bring in resources from the outside it might demoralise and cause resentment among the people doing good work already.

When you start with what works, you avoid all these risks. And if you do then decide to bring in outside resources to further your efforts, you do so from a base of knowledge. You're much more likely to get good results.

What's Your Organisation's Capability for Starting with What Works?

Most organisations have huge reserves of hidden wealth. I help organisations take perspectives they don't normally take, and see opportunities they don't normally see. Then I help them seize those opportunities, which can lead to huge productivity increases without capital investment.

How capable is your organisation of starting with what works? Figure 1.1 provides a way for you to assess yourself.

There is a questionnaire for each of the two dimensions, below.

	LO	HI
HI Ability to exploit potential	Wasted talent	Productive value creation
	Missed opportunity	
LO	Heading for extinction	Perpetual dreamer

Ability to discover potential

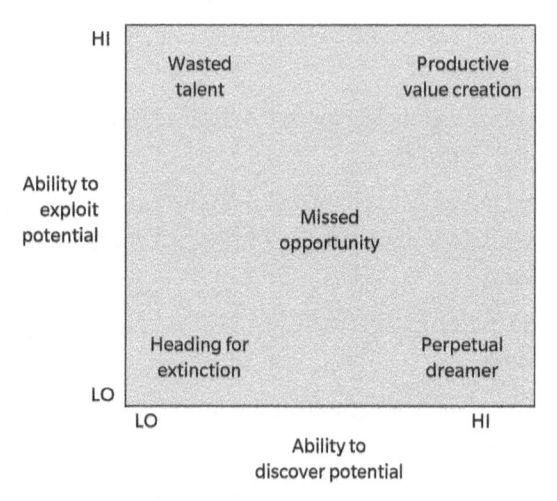

Figure 1.1 Ability to start with what works

Ability to discover potential

Below is a checklist for you to assess your organisation's ability to uncover hidden potential:

	Agree	Disagree
1. People focus on customer results, not just products, processes and technology.	❏	❏
2. Employees seek out unarticulated needs of customers.	❏	❏
3. People bring insights from customers to the attention of senior management.	❏	❏
4. If an employee has an idea with potential, that idea will be treated well.	❏	❏
5. People from different parts of the business can figure out if they have pieces of the puzzle that could be of use to their colleagues.	❏	❏
6. Employees co-create new ideas with their customers and suppliers.	❏	❏
7. People who challenge assumptions intelligently are valued and rewarded.	❏	❏
8. The company makes sure to hear from people outside our industry, as advisors, as employees, and as speakers.	❏	❏
9. People are prepared to face complaints and critical feedback from customers.	❏	❏
10. People are often trying ideas out to see if they have traction.	❏	❏

Scoring

1 point for every 'Agree'.

HIGH	10–9	Forward-thinking, mentally agile organisation. Open to new ideas and to challenges assumptions. If you are also excellent at changing so that you can bring these insights to fruition, you will be a world-beater!
MED	8–6	Quite innovative. But there's scope to make a step change of progress.
LOW	5 or less	Stuck in the mud.

Ability to exploit potential

Below is a checklist for you to assess your organisation's ability to exploit uncovered potential:

	Agree	Disagree
1. The organisation has ways to experiment with new combinations of resources.	❏	❏
2. We will consider cannibalising an existing line of business if we think it necessary for long-term sustainability.	❏	❏
3. People prototype things to see what works, rather than having endless debates on the principle of whether things will work.	❏	❏
4. People are used to modifying their roles, teams and assignments.	❏	❏
5. People don't use the excuse, 'I would think strategically, or innovate, but I have too many short-term operational things to do.'	❏	❏
6. People put customer interests ahead of vested interests.	❏	❏
7. Funds can flow to great opportunities, even if unbudgeted at the start of the year.	❏	❏

Why Start with What Works?

	Agree	Disagree
8. There seems to be a rule, standard, code, or 'custodian' that forestalls almost every good idea.	❑	❑
9. We have huge change initiatives, with loads of up-front communication, kick-off meetings, trainings and certifications, but actual results are slow to show up.	❑	❑
10. It is safe, from a career point of view, to pursue a good opportunity that may nonetheless fall short of expectations.	❑	❑

Scoring

Give yourself 1 point for each 'Agree' *except* for questions 8 & 9, where you get a point for 'Disagree'.

HIGH	10–9	You are like the crew of the Enterprise! Make it so, and it happens. With strong insights you will be irresistible. Just make sure you avoid complacency and keep improving.
MED	8–6	Like many organisations, you have scope to improve your agility.
LOW	5 or less	Always on the wrong foot.

Your return on investment (ROI): hidden wealth from hidden gold

Think about your company. Of all the opportunities you had to manifest hidden wealth yesterday, what percentage do you think you seized? Think about it: even if you are operating well, if you're only finding 75% of the opportunities and you only exploit them to 60%, you could have a huge productivity jump if you just looked at things differently.

How Do You Start with What Works?

Here's a preview of ten principles I have found to apply across the widest range of situations, in sectors as diverse as manufacturing, media, technology, universities, construction and financial services.

As we look at each principle in the course of the book, we'll see examples you can think about and discuss with your team. These are evocative of the 'start with what works' mindset, and invariably trigger fruitful discussions and insights.

But then we'll get even more specific, and discuss tools and templates you can use to look with fresh eyes at the resources you already have. You'll learn how to apply them to the situations you face, so that you can identify new opportunities, and turn those opportunities into action.

Principle One: Recombine existing elements so they create more value

You can practice a kind of business alchemy. The alchemists attempted to create gold by recombining basic elements. Their idea was to create something of greater value not by adding something new, but by remixing what was already there. In a way, successful record producers, literary editors and sports coaches can be seen as being involved in a kind of alchemy. So can business leaders. Like Cardinal Health and MAN Trucks, you can often recombine and repackage existing elements to solve a bigger, more valuable problem, and do it in a way that has favourable economics both for the customer and for you. We'll look at a number of tools to help, including *The Carwash Technique* and *Profit Amplification*.

Principle Two: Escape from fixed purposes

For reasons we'll review in Chapter 2 – including a tendency to see resources in terms of fixed purposes – we can easily overlook hidden resources that could serve as platforms for growth. In this chapter, we'll see how some companies like Amazon Web Services, Lotus Cars and LEGO have utilised hidden resources to achieve fast and profitable growth they hadn't even anticipated during their earlier business planning. We'll use a tool called the *Hidden Resource Inventory* to scan for hidden resources and clarify the platform for growth that you may already have but be overlooking.

Principle Three: Reverse engineer yourself

In this chapter, we'll be drilling deeper into the details of your own unique vault of what I call your *implied* resources. An implied resource is something that logically must be there for the things you do to work. I find that people often overlook or discount these resources. We'll see how to use the thinking patterns of computer programmers to uncover implied resources, and look at how they can be applied to create growth and reinvention, even in tricky circumstances.

Principle Four: Let the world teach you

In this fast-moving world, beware of grand plans laden with unwarranted assumptions. Even plans resting on highly plausible analysis regularly turn out to be ungrounded. Pursuing such plans wastes a lot of resources. Yet if you ask the world the right way, it will teach you what works, giving you a confident basis for scaling things up. So use what you already have to test your assumptions before you waste money. This chapter will show you how, like Zappos and others using disciplined experimentation, you can identify the key assumptions which could sink a business idea and test them in the real world as early and cheaply as possible.

Principle Five: Watch what actually happens

Customers are often unable to articulate their needs or predict their buying behaviour in imagined scenarios – a fact that limits the value of traditional market research. When Disney launched their stores, they built a realistic mock-up on a spare movie lot, invited people in, and watched what actually happened. This unfiltered approach – using existing resources – provided much better information than externally commissioned interview responses. Marriott followed a similar path in developing their time-share villas, achieving higher revenues from smaller spaces than predicted. You can similarly find or set up situations to discover valuable insights from what actually happens.

Principle Six: Find the few things that really make a difference

Experts can easily fall into a trap: they build products and design services based on their own view of what is required and end up adding features the customer doesn't appreciate. Companies like GE are working to avoid such over-engineering. They ask: 'Where are we working hard to deliver things that the customer isn't noticing, or simply doesn't care about? Could we do better on the 'less is more' principle?' We'll look at tools to identify factors that make the real difference.

Principle Seven: Use very plain words to describe how you want things to be

As your offerings change, your organisation will have to keep up. When people are talking about a change that's needed in their organisation, they bandy about words like *transformation, communication* and *engagement* and everyone nods. But what the heck do these words mean? Unless you get really clear, you'll be tempted to buy in generic 'transformation programmes', 'communication trainings' and 'engagement tools'. These generic 'solutions' are often time-consuming and disruptive. They are at best blunt instruments, and at worst, irrelevant to the real issues affecting your business. In contrast, when you describe those issues, and your desired outcomes, in very plain words, many can be sorted out by your own people, with minimal outside assistance. We'll see how the *TV Documentary* technique can lead you to the precise, actionable information you need.

Principle Eight: Look beyond 'Us and Them'

'Us and Them' stories abound inside the organisation. These stories foster attitudes that waste endless time and energy. They are sources of stress and unproductive conflict, and they make it particularly hard to create joined-up experiences for customers. When sales is blaming production, or managers are blaming employees, and everybody is blaming IT or finance, it's much tougher to bring fresh ideas for using existing resources to fruition. We'll look at both direct and indirect ways to work with stories in order to challenge assumptions about 'Us and Them', thereby creating conditions for positive change.

Principle Nine: Bring customers inside

Most companies talk a good game about being customer-centric, but even the best ones perform patchily. The customer-centric leader has to deal with the fact that it's natural for employees to think of customers as being 'outside' the business. After all, in physical terms, they don't live in your buildings (they come into retail outlets of course, but only as visitors from the outside, and they rarely show up at head office, the call centre or the factory). Significant numbers of employees, regardless of level, rarely if ever meet a customer in person. To the extent customer-facing staff get replaced by chatbots, this will become even more true.

Your customers know more about what they will buy than you do, but their views are often barely known to employees. Sometimes those views are even dismissed by the company's technical experts who think, 'What can I learn from *them*?' Businesses as different as McCain and Lego have benefited from bringing insights from their existing customers into the very centre of their companies. We'll look at ways you can do that too.

Principle Ten: Give control to get control

As they seek to execute their plans, leaders flit between two troublesome stances: micromanagement and 'Somehow Management.' The former limits the organisation's awareness to those things the leader knows of personally – a debilitating constraint. The latter substitutes magical thinking for rationality – that easily leads to an uncoordinated mess. A breakthrough leadership strategy needs to balance management control and staff autonomy. To pull this off, we'll learn from military strategy, including the *REWARDS* format for delegating missions.

In Summary: Here's the Plan

I hope I've excited you about the hidden gold waiting to be discovered and exploited. Here's what's ahead:

The ten principles in depth

In Chapters 3–12, we'll look at each of the Start with what works principles in detail, with plenty of exercises, frameworks and questions to consider with your team.

Getting started, releasing change

Chapter 13 will save you time and smooth your path. As you start to apply the Ten Principles, you'll be making changes in your organisation. We'll look at why you should be cautious about driving change, and instead learn to *release* it. We'll also see why, though the timing never seems ideal, the best time to start is right now.

Making it personal: you go first

The best way to grasp the idea of starting with what works is to apply it to yourself. This is equally true whether you're an established leader or an ambitious individual contributor. In the Epilogue, I'll show you how to apply start with what works to take your personal strategy to the next level.

Additional resources

The e-Appendix – at *bassclusker.com/swww* – provides further help in applying the start with what works approach in your organisation.

Before we meet those principles, though, let's look at how people block themselves from noticing their business's hidden potential.

Chapter 2

How We Miss Hidden Potential

A few years ago I would have been surprised to be writing a book called *Start with What Works*. The notion would have sounded obvious. But if you look at what actually happens in organisations, you'll see that managers often start with what *doesn't* work. And from one point of view, it makes sense. Managers need to be good problem solvers: that means they are looking for what is not working so they can run in and solve it. But although they succeed in solving those problems and therefore keeping the show on the road, they may be reinforcing a mindset of limited expectations.

Here's what I mean. Given a problem, the job is to get everything back the way it was. The hidden assumption is that yesterday's standard is the gold standard. Perhaps people would question that assumption if they felt they had the time, but they neglect to because they're so busy making sure stuff gets done. That's a shame, because another look at the assumption could be time well spent.

You can't ignore (most) problems. But a habitual focus on what's *not* working makes managers miss hidden resources and the potential contained therein. To release that potential, it is necessary to first look for and promote examples of what *is* working.

In particular, you need to be vigilant for positive anomalies: situations where results are out of proportion to what you'd expect for the effort. For example, the guy with his feet up on the desk who nonetheless seems to make the most sales, or one particular customer who is – inexplicably – sending you disproportionate amounts of referral business. These anomalies are clues to better results without extra time and effort.

It's Already Happening Somewhere: Find and Utilise What Is Working

Most organisations could call on overlooked resources that would make a tremendous difference to them. The trouble is that they can't always find their way to those resources. It's as if they've forgotten that they have them. In this way, organisational memory is like individual memory: *we have access to much more than we remember.*

To see what I mean, let me ask you a question: have you ever flicked back through your holiday photos and rediscovered events that you had forgotten, even though they happened quite recently? It's not that you had exactly forgotten these events, but you wouldn't have remembered them, either, if it weren't for the prompts.

I find that my clients have a similarly selective amnesia. It shows up all the time in my work with them. It's a source of repeated surprise and delight to find that a client has already done the thing, or has the knowledge, that – if reapplied or reconfigured – would transform their situation.

For example, I was working with an entrepreneur who wanted to validate a business idea before spending too much time and money on it. To do that, he needed to find and speak with a specific type of difficult-to-reach 'senior executive.' To listen to him, getting such a person to give him their time would be almost as hard as building the business itself. I enquired – forensically, to his irritation – into the characteristics he was seeking.

'They'd be a top-level finance executive of a substantial business – at least $1 billion in revenues – who was not just concerned with compliance or costs, but was genuinely prepared to support innovation across their business.'

'What else?' I asked.

'They wouldn't just be paying lip-service to doing new things: they'd really mean it.'

'What else?'

'For goodness sake, I don't know. Er . . . they'd have the authority to take action and the clout to make it stick.'

'What else?'

'Andy, you are starting to irritate me! Erm . . . they'd be intellectually curious enough to listen to how my idea might help them, and . . . *wait a minute!* I met someone like that only last week at a university alumni event. He's based in Hong Kong. I'll email him!'

It still fascinates me. How could this entrepreneur have forgotten that he knew exactly the person he needed *already*? I find that this kind of thing happens all the time, but most people don't seem to notice it.

When we're too focused on short-term targets, or ironically, too driven by 'productivity systems', our attention narrows and we lose access to things we know. This hard-charging entrepreneur needed to stop and think. Once he took a new perspective, he realised he had the answer already.

Just as individuals forget what they know, so do organisations. I worked with a divisional vice president who needed to increase sales to large existing customers in a hurry. His team's discussions had settled into a rut: all they could think of was to launch new – unspecified – products, recruit additional salespeople, or both. Not very original, but not unreasonable either. The problem was, the business cases were yet to be made and, even assuming approval, the actual implementation was going to be too slow to hit his assigned target.

We looked at the issue afresh and concluded that what actually could work in time was a new 'customer intimacy' programme. This programme would take advantage of my client's position in the market, enabling them to provide valuable insights and exclusive connections for customers in exchange for a recurring subscription.

'You mean it would be like this programme we designed in 2012?' said a colleague.

With the groundwork already done, the programme was implemented in three months.

When you flick back through holiday photos, it re-evokes positive memories. That's the whole idea on which Kodak and Polaroid built their businesses. It's not that we've forgotten the memories – it's just that we don't remember them. Similarly, more often than you think, it's not that you don't have the ability to achieve something, it's that you don't remember that you do.

Many of the principles we'll meet in the following chapters are designed to re-evoke your knowledge of resources you have already.

Reasons We Overlook What We Have Already

Starting with what works can feel odd for managers who have achieved success by being problem solvers. The problem with problem solving is that you move things back to status quo, rather than advancing the action. In contrast, when you start with what works, you're not only fixing things but you're potentially opening up whole new avenues, based on your strengths and the resources that you already have. But if this is such a great idea, why don't more organisations do it? Let's look at some of the mindsets responsible.

1. We're seduced by the idea of a saviour

Frequently, managers overlook resources they have at hand, and instead, they look outside for one-shot solutions. They're hoping that something or someone from the outside will bring in a kind of magic bullet that's going to do all the work. That doesn't usually happen.

One of the most common ways managers look too quickly to the outside for help is in trying to buy in, what I call, a saviour solution. These managers assume that a saviour has some special knowledge or ability that no one inside the organisation has. Here's an example of a typical saviour:

> **The Rockstar Hire.** They arrive with a fanfare and a burnished track record. They race in to rearrange the deckchairs. They fail to appreciate the existing talent, teamwork and achievements of their new colleagues. Their mantra is, 'When I was at Google/Apple/Amazon/Goldman Sachs/_____ (fill in the blank) we did *this*.' Research shows that these Rockstar Hires often disappoint, mainly because their previous success, though real, was not just down to them. They rode a wave created by teamwork, slick processes, great product–market fit and talented colleagues.

Of course, saviours don't have to appear in human form. Here are two examples of inanimate saviour solutions:

> **The Acquisition.** It's easy for bosses to find themselves sequestered in the corner office with only their bankers to talk to. There, they lose touch with the actual business – with their employees and customers. Their world is reduced to a bunch of spreadsheets. And so the answer to the question, 'How do I grow?' is naturally, 'Do a deal. Buy something.' It's exciting to be a deal-maker! But once you've bought a business, you have to integrate it. And to do that, you better know a lot about the strangers you call your employees and your customers.

> **The New IT System.** How many times have you heard someone say that the answer to the company's challenges is a new

customer relationship management (CRM) system, a new enterprise resource planning (ERP) system, or these days especially, some artificial intelligence (AI)? To listen to the proponents of these systems you would think getting the thing set up will be a breeze, after which everyone will enthusiastically embrace their changed work routines, leading to guaranteed success. But it rarely seems to go as smoothly in practice.

Don't get me wrong. I'm all for hiring the best talent, intelligent deal making and benefiting from the intelligent use of technology. The problem lies in seeing these things as saviours, because saviours often turn out to have feet of clay. In fact, 'rockstar' hires, mergers & acquisitions and showcase IT projects are among the highest-risk things business leaders can rely on.

2. We copy the wrong things from the outside, rather than seeking the right things within

Businesses copy each other too much. It might be from a desire for safety in numbers, an obsession with 'industry best practices', or simple laziness. There is no law saying that your call centre message needs to say, 'Your call is important to us,' yet everyone's does.

Of course it can make sense to copy successful performers, but only if you copy the things that make the difference. It's easy to look at successful performers and draw the wrong conclusions about the causes of their success. I once heard this put graphically as follows: All CEOs go to the toilet, but nobody thinks that is a common factor in their career success as business leaders.

This is a potential problem for all business books that hold up successful companies as exemplars. That includes my book, of course, which is why I recommend that you check that lessons from others actually apply to you (see Chapter 6, 'Let The World Teach You'). Examples are great for inspiration and as a source of idea you can test, but not as models to be blindly followed.

3. We don't notice the familiar

On my way home I often have to stop at the same set of traffic lights. The first time I was stuck at those lights, my attention was caught by an unusual sign. It said UTCHE.

That confused me momentarily. I thought, 'What is UTCHE? – is it a foreign language – maybe something Germanic? Is it a brand name? Or a type of shop?'

These questions flashed through my mind almost instantaneously. There was that moment of confusion, of novelty. A bit like when you wake up in a hotel room and you're not sure where you are for a moment. And then I realised what was going on. The sign used to say BUTCHER. But the letters B and R had fallen off.

Now, when the letters first fell off, the butcher probably noticed. Even if he didn't, someone almost certainly came into the shop and said, 'Oi, Mate. The letters have fallen off your sign.' And the butcher really meant to get the sign fixed. But he was busy. He procrastinated. A few days went by and he didn't get round to it. Pretty soon he stopped noticing that sign at all.

Now if the butcher crossed the street and looked at his shop from the other side, the way it would appear to a prospective customer, then: WHAM! It would hit him in the face. It would be a really clear signal that he could use to better run his business.

But he walks by it every day and isn't even aware of it. He's not aware that it's putting prospective customers off. And so his business bumbles along.

I'm not having a go at that butcher. It's easy to have this sort of thing happen. We probably all have similar things at home: a toilet roll holder that fell off, a scratch on a floor, a bent light shade you meant to replace, an 'urgent' Post-it note on a computer screen that's been there for three months.

You see these things, in the sense that the light hits your retina, but you no longer perceive them. It's very human.

How many of these signals are we missing – at home or in our businesses? It's really hard to say. Unless you can somehow figure out a way to take the perspective you get 'on the other side of the street' – the prospective customer's point of view – you will be oblivious to these things.

4. We get caught up in a dream world

Nick Bostrom, a philosopher from Oxford, and Elon Musk, everybody's favourite example of an entrepreneur these days, both seriously seem to believe we are living in a computer simulation like the one in the film, *The Matrix*.

It sounds a bit bonkers to me. But that doesn't mean I disagree with the idea that we live in a world of illusion. Businesses as well as individuals have to strive to remain in contact with reality – or else.

When I became a consultant, the first lesson my mentor taught me was to be mindful to deal with 'observable behaviour and evidence in the environment.' It's wise advice for all business people – hearsay and mistaken beliefs can easily send you in the wrong direction.

It's very easy to get caught up in convincing illusions.

One morning, while walking in the park near where I live, I saw a magpie standing on the grass. Nothing unusual in that – they're very common in that park. What was unusual was that as I got nearer to it, it transformed into a shiny black bin bag! The effect was so striking that I laughed out loud at the trick my mind had played.

A psychologist might explain that perception is largely constructed from a mixture of memories and expectations. I expect to see magpies in the park, and so given a plausible signal, I saw a magpie.

This then got me wondering: what if I hadn't got close enough to discover the bin bag? I would have known that I had seen a magpie, for sure. And yet I would have been completely mistaken.

And there's another layer of illusion once you consider the effect of beliefs. In England at least, the number of magpies one encounters is the subject of superstition. This is captured in the rhyme: 'One for sorrow, two for joy, three for a girl, and four for a boy.' So if I were superstitious, I wouldn't just have seen a bird, I'd have seen an omen!

Maybe this would colour the rest of the day. I'd see innocent coincidences as threats. Maybe I'd overlook opportunities, dismissing them as too good to be true. Maybe I'd dwell on perceived weaknesses in myself and others, while disregarding strengths.

What are some of the convincing illusions business people can get caught up in? Well, for example, that:

- Their customers are only interested in price (but they're often not).
- Customers won't pay more (but they often will).
- Generation X, Y, Z want everything on a plate (but they often don't).
- Their products are average but it doesn't matter because 'our service is excellent' (but customers find the service department arrogant and uncaring).
- What gets measured gets done (but what gets measured often gets gamed).

These illusions are convincing: they seem real!

All of us can get caught out by this stuff. That's why we need ways to escape the bewitching effect of what we think we know.

5. We won't accept prophets in their own land

Too many managers overlook the staff's views, and therefore cut themselves off from a vast store of potential for business improvement.

Sometimes, regrettably, they are deliberately dismissive, seeing frontline people as less qualified and of lower status in the pecking order. 'What can they know?' they ask themselves. More often though, the bias is unconscious – it simply doesn't occur to executives to consider whether the frontline might have valuable insights and ideas.

Whatever the causes, the tendency is damaging. One turnaround specialist says that the first thing he does when called in to rescue a failing business is to talk to the shopfloor and customer service people to find out 'how management have messed up the business, and what we should do to fix it.'

The answers are almost always valuable. Time and again, the information to help the business has been there all along, but was ignored by managers.

People on the frontline know about customers, they know about waste, and they know about bottlenecks. How well do you tap into that knowledge?

6. Exotica from afar distract us from what we have

Justin Haber is a professional footballer from Malta. He is also the owner of a restaurant that featured on the Netflix business turn-around series 'Restaurants on The Edge'. Haber is a fanatic about seafood. Consequently, he was flying in the finest oysters from Normandy, langoustine from Norway and so on. As you can imagine, his costs were astronomical, as were his losses. What was bizarre was this: just 100 metres from his harbour-front restaurant was a seafood market selling superb Mediterranean produce caught that day. How is it possible that he could have overlooked this?

Maybe you could just say Haber is a better footballer than restaurateur. But I think the issue is not so much about acumen as perception. Normandy oysters and Norwegian langoustine have cachet, amplified by being sourced somewhere else. If you're from Malta, they seem more exotic than the produce at the local fish market.

The word 'exotic' literally means 'from the outside'. The expert from afar is more appealing than the prophet from our own land. I once heard a New Yorker confess that while he'd never visited the Statue of Liberty, he couldn't wait to get to Paris to see the Eiffel Tower. Stuff from outside just *seems* more valuable, whether or not it actually is.

7. We get stuck in existing categories

The Platypus is a strange creature found in eastern Australia. Like many reptiles, it lays eggs instead of giving birth to live young. But unlike a reptile, it is warm-blooded. The bizarre appearance of this egg-laying, venomous, duck-billed, beaver-tailed, otter-footed mammal baffled European naturalists when they first encountered it. Some considered it an elaborate fraud – they thought that tricky taxidermists had sewn a duck's beak onto the body of a beaver.

Is a Platypus a mammal or a reptile? How can such an 'anomaly' (the *Brisbane Times* recently called it 'a genetic mongrel') exist? Such questions are not relevant to the Platypus of course, which has been thriving for millions of years without the warrant of some Victorian naturalist from London, or newspaper hack from Brisbane.

When observed facts do not fit in with existing categories, people struggle. They resist the facts, or just explain them away. This is a huge trap for 'industry experts.' Think about the way the major US automakers responded to early 'compact' Japanese imports in the 1970s. They basically said: 'Call that a car?' and carried on building gas-guzzlers. This is the same mindset that predicted doom when Alan Mulally was appointed CEO at Ford. They 'knew' that you couldn't run a US car company unless you were 'a car guy', and Mulally was from aviation, having been a senior executive at Boeing. He responded by engineering a dramatic turnaround, pursuing a global strategy substantially based, as it happens, on a compact platform. The company's performance in 2010 was its best in a decade. Maybe those 'industry insiders' would benefit from some practice in allowing new ideas to re-jig their tired old categories?

8. We dismiss positive anomalies and outliers because we rely on statistical summaries

My clients know I am fond of the following joke: 'Did you hear the one about the statistician who drowned crossing a river of an average depth of two feet?' Averaging makes large amounts of information easier to grasp, but it can hide the most useful and critical data points. There are so many applications of this insight that it is well worth developing the habit of treating all averages with suspicion. Here's just one example:

FT.com on May 24, 2013 carried an interesting article by David Oakley, Investment Correspondent. It was entitled 'Time to buy Europe's world-beating shares'. It starts as follows: 'It is a fact that might cause a few raised eyebrows. Some of Europe's world-beating companies and stocks are domiciled in the very countries commonly regarded as the eurozone's laggards. From a Spanish sausage skin maker to an Irish betting group and Italian fashion business, the eurozone's economically challenged periphery is the base for some of the best-performing stocks anywhere in the world.' Do read the original article for the company examples which include Viscofan, a Spanish sausage skin maker, Inditex, the Spanish fashion retailer that owns Zara, and Salvatore Ferragamo, the Italian clothing and accessories company.

There is an extremely important reminder in this story: when people talk about 'the economy', they are doing so on the average. Individual companies may have much higher growth than the GDP growth of the country they are in, or the growth of the industrial sector or market they are in. Similarly, individual companies may also have dramatically higher profitability than their sector average.

Averages can mask similar effects inside companies, too. Sometimes one team, or one shop, or one manufacturing cell, or one individual may have outlying performance that is hidden by the statistics. For example, my friend Alastair Dryburgh,[1] author of *Everything You Know About Business is Wrong*, was once appointed Commercial Director of a marketing consultancy. The business had been putting huge effort into trying to raise its profitability. Alastair calculated the consultancy's *average* profit per hour. It was £120. Then he looked at the detail. Some projects were earning as much as £300 per hour, while others only earned £30! Yet without this analysis, it looked as if all the consultants were contributing equally. Simply by stopping taking on certain types of unprofitable projects and zeroing in on the profitable types, he was able to raise average profit per hour by 25% in nine months.

It we let our alertness slip, it's easy to be lulled into the assumption that we are at the mercy of what are, after all, abstractions: 'the economy', 'GDP', 'consumer sentiment'. I'm not saying these convey no information, but they don't always contain much of use. I often hear economic indicators being used to create compelling-sounding rationales for battening down the hatches, where other companies sailing in the same conditions are making dramatic progress.

Where is best to focus: on depressing abstract summaries, or on specific, concrete, inspiring counter-examples?

9. We 'know' too much about the business

Readers might understandably say: 'I've done well with this business so far. I've got people who know this industry working flat out. I don't believe there is significant extra potential from what is already here. What makes you think there is?'

Paradoxically, extensive experience in a business can make it too easy to overlook the hidden potential therein. As managers develop experience, their expectations for what is possible quickly habituate. They get used to their industry, their organisation and their people. When they look at it, they see possibilities that are only incremental improvements – 'more of the same.' Wise managers need to be alert to this and have tools and practices to see a familiar world in a new light.

> ## Box 2.1
> ### Use vs Utilise
>
> A lot of people treat the words *Use* and *Utilise* as synonyms, but there's actually a useful distinction between their meanings. To *use* something means to employ it in order to achieve an intended purpose. The meaning of *utilise* is subtly different: it means to employ something in a novel way, or for an improvised purpose, as distinct from the one originally intended. *Using* a resource is a matter of business-as-usual. *Utilising* a resource is a matter of innovation. This book suggests adopting a utilisation frame of mind.

In Summary

We've looked at some of the habitual mindsets that get in the way of appreciating what works, and making more of our hidden resources. People forget what they have, they undervalue what they have, and they let shiny objects get in the way, distorting their perceptions.

The good news is that there are antidotes to these habitual mindsets. So in the following chapters, let's take a look at these antidotes: the principles, mindsets and tools that are going to let you create your gold.

Chapter 3

Principle One: Recombine Existing Elements So They Create More Value

It's become a cliché to say that in our turbulent (so-called 'VUCA[1]') world, businesses need constantly to innovate in order to grow and thrive. In my experience, leaders have a number of frustrations in translating that idea into action, including:

1. **The change dilemma.** Just as any experienced therapist has had clients say, 'I want things to be different, but without me having to change', would-be innovation leaders come up against the same challenge.
2. **The 'Day Job' excuse.** People agree to pursue new initiatives then resist them by saying, 'I would have done more, but I've got

to look after the Day Job.' They thereby position innovation as something *extra*, outside their responsibilities.

3 **The comfort of the familiar.** People fear abandoning actions that have worked in the past, even if they're obviously failing now. They will say, 'We should stick to the proven way, just redouble our efforts.'

4 **The sunk cost fallacy.** People stubbornly back a failing course of action with the economically irrational argument: 'We've come so far, and invested so much money, time, prestige: let's not lose that investment.'

Some leaders will – if they are candid – admit to one or more of these tendencies themselves. They will even more often complain of them to their colleagues.

Pundits often criticise these businesses and their leaders, calling them 'stuck-in-the-mud' or worse. But it's easy to empathise with their predicament. I find that the leaders I talk to almost all accept the need for innovation. They're well aware that competitors converge, making it hard to differentiate. And they don't need reminding that disruptors can emerge from left-field.

But stories from about Silicon Valley 'moonshots' – while inspiring – can sound like pipe-dreams. And even in a corporate environment that is well funded, growth resources are constrained by internal competition (not to mention that if you get the funding, that might be the beginning of your problems: akin to playing roulette with the boss's money).

Wouldn't it be great if there was a way forward that retained familiarity in the midst of change, built on rather than sought to relegate 'the Day Job', didn't simply dismiss past glories, and made it feel like you were recouping at least some return on failed investments rather than having the difficult emotional challenge of writing them off completely?

Starting with what works helps with all of this, and nowhere more so than with this first principle: recombining *existing* elements so they create more value.

Be a Business Alchemist

How do you take commonplace elements – things you have at hand – and create new value? Alchemy provides a provocative metaphor for understanding how to do that. The alchemists' most noteworthy pursuit was the quest to turn base elements, such as lead, into gold. Clearly they failed in that endeavour, yet as far-fetched as their work might sound, it turns out that they had a surprising amount of influence. In fact, the alchemists are now acknowledged as the forerunners of modern scientists. Isaac Newton considered himself an alchemist, and wrote more on the subject than he wrote on physics,[2] and Robert Boyle, the father of modern chemistry, built the science on foundations laid by his alchemical mentors. If you consider the incredible wealth built on the foundations of Newton's physics and Boyle's chemistry, it turns out that – through their combination of ambitious goals, imaginative hypotheses and increasingly rigorous experimentation – the alchemists actually created something of even greater value than gold.

It's important to realise that the alchemists weren't trying to create something from nothing. They were trying to create something more valuable out of what already existed. They weren't trying to do it by magical incantations; they were trying to be scientists, trying to use what they had on hand – lead, mercury and so on – and to work with natural processes.

While the literal ideas of alchemy may not be practical, the following question is still worth thinking about as a provocation:

'How do you take basic elements and turn them into gold?'

Put another, less metaphorical, way:

'How do you take existing resources that you have at hand, and turn them into something far more valuable?'

The answer starts by identifying the basic elements in your business and then experimenting in order to understanding how the way they are recombined can influence their value. Let's look at an example of how this can work.

Alchemy at Cardinal Health: turning 'commodities' into dramatic new value

Cardinal Health was stuck. One of its businesses manufactured surgical supplies – things like gloves, sutures and scalpels – and it was watching its margins vanish. The company was experiencing intense price competition because hospitals regarded their excellent quality products as commodities that were essentially interchangeable with those of other suppliers. It was getting harder and harder to make a profit, and they were thinking of getting out of the business altogether.

But before taking that final step, someone decided to pay renewed attention to how the products were actually being used. In the terms we will meet in the next chapter, they tapped into their overlooked relationship resources – the contacts they had built up with the hospitals – to access the know-how and experience of the surgeons, nurses and administrators involved.

This might seem an obvious move in hindsight – it's just, 'Talk to your customers,' right? But it's not what you *actually* see people do in the heat of intense competition. After all, faced with the attention-narrowing effects of pressure, it's easy to succumb to Dive Bomber syndrome: locking on to cost-reduction targets and failing to notice the wider environment while flying into the ground. As a rule, excellent operating executives are promoted because they can get large numbers of people to work together to hit short-term targets. They often find it harder to widen their fields of view, challenge basic assumptions and release new opportunities (in fact, helping them to do that has been the primary reason for the Executive Education programmes I've run at business schools).

Cardinal Health was at a crossroads with the surgical equipment business – however competently operated, it was obvious that business as usual was no longer enough. Therefore, they did tap into their relationship resources. In doing so, they hit on an extremely powerful idea: bundling supplies into kits that were perfectly matched to specific surgical procedures. So, for example, for a hernia operation, they would deliver a kit on the day of the operation, with all the basic elements sequenced correctly in sterile packs. This had the effect of simplifying setup, minimising risks of error and stock outages, and so helped reduce hospital inventory and inventory management costs. With the same basic products, insight into their customers' real needs, and well-thought-out packaging, they achieved dominance and earned a well-deserved premium by creating more from what was already working.

Cardinal Health had found an idea that an alchemist might have found fascinating. In a sense the company had indeed turned base elements into gold.

Cardinal Health's transmutation of value

Cardinal Health broke their range of offerings down into its most fundamental form and transmuted it into something 'golden'. In short, they started with what was working, including:

- their ability to manufacture high-quality surgical instruments and supplies;
- relationships with doctors who were happy to discuss the way these products were actually being used day to day;
- relationships with hospital administrators which could provide insights into operating theatre economics;
- their abilities to brand, package and ship products.

The basic elements in the Cardinal Health example are the commodity products, such as the sutures and scalpels, together with process know-how about manufacturing, shipping and so on. Figure 3.1 identifies some of these, together with a description of the value of each element. It's a useful exercise to repeat this for your own business.

Notice that Cardinal Health organised these elements so that the combined value exceeded the sum of the parts: *that's* the alchemy. Let's look in more detail at how that works.

Element	Value
Scalpel	Enables surgeon to make clean, accurate incisions
Sutures	Enables surgeon to close wounds
Surgical gloves	Allows surgical team to operate without infecting patient
Delivery to order	Enables hospital staff to maximise their time working with patients
Packaging	Protects the product until its ready to be used

Figure 3.1 Breaking down offerings into value elements

Base versus alchemical value

Figure 3.2 contrasts 'base' with 'alchemical' value. Each of the numbered lines represents a different way of thinking – a different mindset – about the relationship between input and output, between effort and results. My observation is that many managers have the mindset represented by line 1. They expect that the more you put in, the more you get out, but only in proportion. This is the commodity

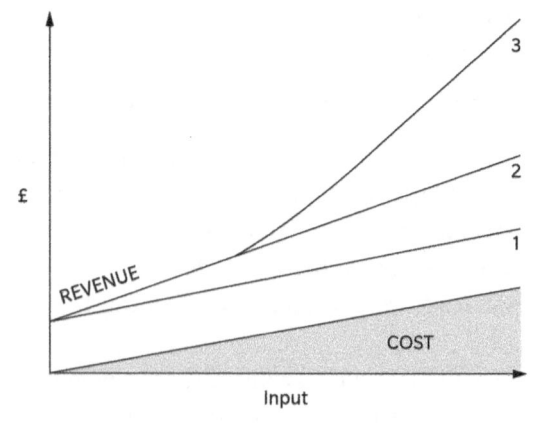

Figure 3.2 Base vs alchemical value

mindset, the ones that says, 'to make more money we need to sell more scalpels.'

Lines 2 and 3 are more interesting, describing highly desirable situations in which value increases disproportionately to costs.

You Can't Polish Lead

I have worked with many businesses that offered top-quality products and services who, struggling to maintain prices in the face of determined competition, could only think of improving quality further – or shouting louder about their superior quality – as a response.

It can be difficult to stand out in a way that's meaningful to customers. Although this can seem an insurmountable problem, it depends how you are looking at it. There may be considerable untapped potential to create value – and therefore raise prices – by taking a fresh look at your offerings and combining existing elements into new combinations, as Cardinal Health did.

It can be hard for engineers and technical experts to accept, but after a certain point further improvements in those base elements won't enable you to keep or win any additional business. In many mature markets, all the competitors may be offering the same quality – at least in the eyes of the customer, which of course is where it matters. For a good example, think about mid-priced family cars, where what's on offer from different manufacturers can be effectively indistinguishable (we'll return for a deeper look at this dimension in Chapter 8 'Find the few things that really make a difference').

For a given tier in a market, offerings – sutures, screen resolutions or legal expertise – are often indistinguishable to the purchasers. Even if they seem quite different to their manufacturers, a car buyer may perceive no important difference between a Vauxhall Astra and a Ford Focus (Again, I'll have more to say about differences that make a difference in Chapter 8).

So what can you do? One answer you often hear is: 'We'll compete by giving superior service.' But service standards can often be matched by competitors too. Is the RAC roadside service really that different from the AA equivalent? Is BA's transatlantic business class really that different from Lufthansa's?

A great way to get started with transmutation is to think about unbundling and rebundling. People like bundles or kits – I think this attraction starts in childhood with birthday and Christmas presents – and if you bundle something appropriately, you amplify its value to the customer disproportionately to your extra input, earning you a price premium above the individual selling prices of the components.

Using Bundles to Transmute Your Business

It's likely that starting with what you have, and perhaps augmenting it with easy-to-come-by extras, you can use intelligent unbundling and re-bundling to make your current offerings more profitable. For example, you can use bundles to:

- reduce the many hassles of using commodity products;
- borrow and transfer emotional appeal from one item to another;
- help people find a rationale for treating themselves;
- introduce something new that the customer might not otherwise have tried;
- educate the buyer about optimal combinations (as a chef does with a tasting menu);
- simply take advantage of the fact that people of all ages like 'kits'.

So, how do you develop such combinations? Six techniques are outlined below.

Bundle method #1. 'Mise en place'

This is a French cookery phrase that means 'putting in place.' It refers to organising and arranging the ingredients and utensils that a chef will require for the dishes they are going to prepare. It's exactly what Cardinal Health did with the surgical kits they tailored to specific operations. By doing the *mise en place* for the surgeons, they commanded a premium.

- Starting with what you already have, plus what you can easily acquire if needed, how can you make it easier for people to set themselves up to make use of your offering?
- Can you advantageously do the *mise en place* for them?

Bundle method #2. 'Before, during and after'

You can use a technique from the theatre to rethink the customer or client experience. Theatre directors sometimes get their cast to improvise what happened immediately before and immediately after the scene actually written by the playwright. That way, they create a backstory which adds depth and makes the scene itself more satisfying. Business can do something similar. For example, Virgin Upper Class does a lot for passengers before and after their flight – food, showers, haircuts, even shoe-shines – and it bumps up the value nicely. It also deepens the passenger's relationship with the brand, leading to repeat business and higher prices.

- How can you make the before, during and after better for your clients and customers?

Bundle method #3. 'While we're doing that for you. . . '

Among many things, Xerox offers document preparation. They noticed that they were being asked to prepare documents in various languages and realised they could offer to do the translation as an integrated service. It's easy and inexpensive to acquire the translation expertise, and the value of that expertise gets amplified by being used in an innovative context. In addition, Xerox get the economies of scale, so can do the translation at a lower cost than their client. More excitingly, they can combine translation with their other capabilities to create new top line value. How about accelerating the roll-out of their clients' new offerings across international markets – for example, translating as well as printing user manuals? That's worth paying for.

- Can you reduce the number of handoffs or subcontractors for your clients to help them get where they need to be more quickly, at lower cost, or with better quality?

Bundle method #4. Borrow some magic

I used to work with an executive development programme director – one who dramatically outsold her peers and built fierce client loyalty – who clearly understood this principle. When she ran a workshop, she would give each delegate a kit of items such as Post-It notes, pens, and so on to accompany the programme notes. She also included a Moleskine notebook.

Now a Moleskine notebook is £15.00–£16.00 – a premium far in excess of its cost of manufacture, earned largely because of the brand. Ryman stationers offer a very nice bound notebook for less than £5.00. But Ernest Hemingway didn't shop at Ryman; he used a Moleskine (at least according to legend), and if that sort of thing matters to you, you will pay the extra.

Compared to the fees for executive development programmes, the Moleskines were almost free. But they created disproportional effects including an instant cachet and making groups feel special, and were more than once an explicit positive talking point among (multiple repeat) buyers.

- Can you borrow some magic from another brand, be it personal or corporate?

Bundle method #5. Dematerialise your products into 'Products-as-a Service' (PaaS)

An increasing number of businesses have stopped thinking about products and services as distinct, recognising that what customers want is a result. That result could come from products, services, or very often from creative blends of the two.³

The idea has actually been around for decades. You've probably heard about Rolls-Royce's 'power by the hour' contracts, which they started offering way back in 1962. In essence Rolls Royce said to aircraft operators, 'You pay for the thrust your aircraft uses, rather than for the engines. We'll monitor the engines and keep them running, so when your pilot adjusts the thrust levers, the right thing always happens.' This removed the operator's engine maintenance burden, while giving Rolls Royce ongoing revenues based on long-term customer relationships.

What is new is that the Internet of Things gives many more businesses the option to offer PaaS. Customers are also much more conditioned to the idea through familiarity with Software-as-as-Service (SaaS) offerings such as Salesforce, Dropbox and Zoom.

In the pure form of PaaS, the manufacturer owns and maintains the product – the customer just uses it. In another scenario, the customer owns the product but is not responsible for keeping it up-and-running.

You can vary the type of value being delivered. For example, a subscription might be priced in terms of particular outcomes, such as hours of uptime or units outputted. Companies such as Caterpillar (mining equipment), Alstom (high-speed trains) and Hilti (construction tools) have all enjoyed success with variations on this theme.

PaaS makes you think about what your customer *really* values. MAN Trucks, working with Hoyer, the fuel distributor business, realised that the cost of the truck itself is only a small part of customers' operating budgets (around 4%). Much bigger influences on profitability include driver absence due to backache, and truck availability at the right location. This suggested various innovations including not only traditional product options such as ergonomic seating, but also the idea of 'truck availability as a service'.

- Can you recast your product offerings in terms of advanced services that meet your customers' needs without involving them in the hassles of ownership?

Bundle method #6. Create aesthetic value through design

I recently attended a tour of the historic Birmingham School of Jewellery, whose director explained a major difference in the pricing of jewellery East to West. In the East, 'bling' jewellery is favoured[4] and the major determinant of price is the breakdown value of the component gems and precious metals. By contrast, in the West, the tendency is to price items based on the value added by the design. This can be far above the value of the broken-down components. In this case, amplification comes from the intangible value of the design, recognising that some combinations of elements are aesthetically or ergonomically more satisfying than others. Apple is of course legendary in its ability to create economic value from design, way out of proportion with the cost of its bills of materials.

- Can you rework your offerings to improve the elegance, ergonomics or artistry they bring to your customers, and so create a premium? It will require more thought than cash.

A Framework for Developing Bundles and Transmuting Value: The Car Wash Paradigm

Once you start searching for ways to take things that are already working and boost their 'alchemical' potential, it helps to have a framework to organise your thinking.

The paradigm – first introduced to me by Alan Weiss as a tool for consulting proposal design – is the familiar Car Wash menu (see Figure 3.3), in which you are presented with a set of base elements, conveniently bundled into (hopefully) coherent options of elevating value.

Principle One: Recombine Existing Elements So They Create More Value

Element \ Bundle	Foam	Rinse	Water blaster	Underbody	Dry	Wax	Value	Price
Gold	*	*	*	*	*	*	Spotless and shiny	£8
Silver	*	*	*	*			Thorough clean	£6
Bronze	*	*					Basic clean	£4

Figure 3.3 'Car Wash' options

Figure 3.4 shows how Cardinal Health looks in the Car Wash framework.

Element \ Bundle	Instruments (Scalpels etc.)	Materials (sutures etc.)	Surgical gloves	Packaging per procedure	Convenient ordering and delivery	Recycling?	Value
Gold	*	*	*	*	*	*	Increased ROI Better reputation
Silver	*	*	*	*	*		No stock-outs No errors More time for nursing Better hygiene
Bronze	*	*	*				High-quality surgical instruments

Figure 3.4 Cardinal Health 'Car Wash' options

Figure 3.5 shows a second example based on the MAN Truck example from above.

45

Start with what works

Element\Bundle	Basic truck	Traditional options (seats etc.)	Predictive maintenance	Repositioning	Autonomous fleet	?	Value
Platinum	*	*	*	*	*	*	Simplified operations, Concentrate on customer, marketing
Gold	*	*	*	*			Smoother cashflow, lower capital requirements, better ROA
Silver	*	*					Relaxed driver, better health and safety, reduced absenteeism
Bronze	*						Reliably deliver for end customers

Figure 3.5 Truck manufacturer 'Car Wash' options

Car Wash Exercise

Here are the steps to using the Car Wash framework to bring alchemical thinking into your business.

1 **Identify your value elements.**
   This is a big subject, and we'll go into it in more detail in the next chapter, under the section 'The hunt for resources.' To get started, though, just break down your offerings into the obvious pieces and see how far you can get (see Figure 3.6). That is often sufficient to come up with some really promising ideas, and it's always a good preamble to a deeper scan, because it can help your team to get the idea without getting bogged down in nuances.

2 **Draw out a template for developing options.**
   If you are working with a team, it's good to copy out the framework shown in Figure 3.7 onto a whiteboard, real or virtual.

Principle One: Recombine Existing Elements So They Create More Value

Bundle \ Base element	1	2	3	4	5	6	Value to customer	Price
3. Gold								
2. Silver								
1. Bronze								

Figure 3.6 Identifying your value elements

Element	Value

Figure 3.7 Template for developing 'Car Wash' options

3 List your base elements along the top of the framework.
Remember to include elements that add value, but that you don't charge for.

4 Make a preliminary attempt to assemble them into coherent bundles.

5 Fill in gaps. Is there anything extra you would need to provide to make the bundles hang together?

You may already have had a breakthrough at this point. But the real alchemy usually happens as you refine the bundles further. To do this, ask yourself the following questions:

1 Does the value of each higher option increase faster than the cost?
2 How far can we top our initial ideas?
3 Do the elements of each option support each other?
4 Are we offering simple, clear choices?

Let's look at these steps in more detail.

47

How to Refine Your Bundles

1. Make sure your bundles create profit amplification

Whenever I have run bundle development sessions, I have observed a dangerous path. People get very enthusiastic about offering more and more to the customer, but in a way that will exhaust the resources of the business. That's just the equivalent of turning lead into more lead.

Remember the diagram we saw in Figure 3.2, contrasting 'base' with 'alchemical' value.

It's vital to ensure amplification: to make sure that the value of each higher option increases faster than the cost.

> ## Box 3.1
> ### Profit amplification
>
> If you go to a rock concert, you'll see impressive banks of speakers all around the stage, even suspended dramatically from the rafters. A good PA ('public address') system takes the input provided by the band and combines it with a different, easily obtained, form of energy: electricity. Without changing the music's essential character, the PA makes the band much louder, so they can sell more tickets. From a business point of view, what's interesting is that the extra energy is much cheaper per hour than a rock star. The PA amplifies not only the band's sound, but their profit too.

The critical aspect of alchemy through bundling is to find ways to take your basic product or service, and by adding the right sort of boost, amplify its profit disproportionately. If there's no amplification, it's not really alchemy.

What are the implications for your bundle development? Recall the six bundle methods. How many can you apply? Don't just throw in more elements or features. Ensure that there is extra value to the customer disproportionate to your additional costs.

2. Push yourself to top your initial ideas: what about Options 4, 5 and 6?

You don't have to present your offerings in the marketplace as a menu of options, but whether you do so, or simply offer the best idea you come up with, the bundling exercise is a valuable spur to innovation. As you move up each level, you are challenging yourself and your team to further understand the potential in the base elements and the way they might impact on your customer. There is no reason to stop at Option 3. Challenge yourselves to develop Options 4, 5 and 6 (or, say, Platinum, Palladium, Rhodium). It's a powerful provocation to come up with step-change offerings.

3. Ensure elements support each other

Rory Sutherland, Vice-Chairman of Ogilvy & Mather UK (and author of *Alchemy: The Surprising Power of Ideas That Don't Make Sense*,[5] a fascinating book which takes another spin on the alchemy metaphor), told me how smart bundling worked for a luxury car manufacturer. Luxury cars are offered with multiple options. But from a buyer's point of view, the most desirable options are sometimes the hardest to justify. For example, few people really need an enhanced sports suspension kit. They may want it, but feel a bit guilty about ordering it. But bundle it with a 'sensible' option like rear parking sensors, and you have an attractive option that people are comfortable buying.

4. Offer simple choices

If you do decide to offer a menu of options, there is a final consideration to keep in mind: it's what the behavioural economists call the *choice architecture* of your offerings. It hits home best if you think about your own experiences as a customer.

It's easy to be overwhelmed by the range of options available to us these days. As Barry Schwarz points out in his book, *The Paradox of Choice*, very often, 'More is *less*.'[6] This is a problem for businesses for two reasons. Firstly, it can be a huge cognitive effort to make any choice at all: how often, faced by multiple confusing options, have you just found it easier to walk away? Secondly, when you make a choice from among unclear options, you are more likely to second-guess yourself and wonder if you should have chosen differently. That's hardly a recipe for satisfaction.

Here's how friends of mine at *#ogilvychange* reworked the choices for potential subscribers to *The Times* newspaper, using a mixture of behavioural economics insight and creative intuition.

The 'Before' choice architecture offered potential subscribers six packs to choose from:

- Digital pack: £4 per week
- Web pack: £2 per week
- 7-day pack: £6 per week
- Weekday pack: £4 per week
- Weekend pack: £4 per week
- Sunday pack: £2 per week

Faced with the 'before' architecture, people were overloaded, opting not to make a decision at all, and instead to do something else. However, when presented with the far simpler 'after' architecture they felt much more comfortable about making a choice.

The 'After' architecture offered three options. All options allowed you to read both *The Times* and *The Sunday Times* on your desktop and your smart phone. You then had three choices on top of that base:

1 access on a tablet;
2 the physical newspapers;
3 tablet and newspapers.

When implemented on the website, this configuration was dramatically effective, with sales of the Ultimate Pack – option 3 – 129% over forecast. So look over your menu and make sure each option is discretely different. And if you want to be absolutely sure, observe people actually trying to decide which option they want – are they clear on the choices available to them, or are they too confused to make a decision?

Concluding Thought: Remember That Value Is in the Eye of the Beholder

One of the great things about attempting to transmute your business is that it forces you to think of value *as perceived by the customer*. It's a fantastic way of getting your people to think like customers, too – because customers don't think about your offerings the way you do.

When my niece was around five years old, my brother told me that given the choice she would rather have an 'OK' doll with a little plastic hairbrush, mirror, shoes and hat, than a better doll – more lifelike, of more costly materials – but with no accessories. An adult might judge the more lifelike doll as 'better,' but the first doll, though cheaper to manufacture, is more fun to play with.

It's a nice example of value alchemy, and it emphasises the point that the value of your offerings is in the eye of the beholder.

The value of practicing business alchemy

The alchemy of recombining existing elements offers:

- Increased differentiation – because by finding imaginative new uses for what you already do well you can generate uniqueness that's hard to copy.
- Growth without needing to raise large amounts of new money – because we're aiming to reuse existing investment in new ways.
- Lower costs of finding new customers – because you already have customers for the elements you are going to build on.

- Faster results – because it's easier to reach customers, and you're basing your new offering on resources that are already to hand.
- Greater return on existing assets – almost by definition.
- Greater reusable learning – the whole process leads to the creation of new assets in a virtuous circle.

We've seen here how you can practice a kind of alchemy by recombining your existing resources to produce more valuable combinations. Let's now deepen our hunt for those resources.

Chapter 4

Principle Two: Escape from Fixed Purposes

As we saw in Chapter 2, habitual mindsets cause us to miss incredibly valuable resources. It's as if those resources are hiding in the background. We *could* see them, but often they stay at a level of unconsciousness. That said, there are ways to look at a business that will reveal a cornucopia of resources that could be turned into innovation, distinctiveness and productivity.

Nature versus Purpose

The originator of the scientific method, Francis Bacon, pointed out that you can think about a technology either in terms of its nature or its purpose.[1] We often think about resources in terms of fixed purposes. An everyday example is provided by baking soda. 'What's the purpose of baking soda?' is a strange question. It's *baking*, obviously. But what if I ask you these questions:

> 'What's the purpose of sodium bicarbonate (the chemical people *call* baking soda)?

And,

'Given the nature of sodium bicarbonate, what else can you do with it?'

It turns out that this molecule – known to chemists even more abstractly as $NaHCO_3$ – can do all kinds of other things apart from helping with baking. See Box 4.1.

Baking soda is the product, but $NaHCO_3$ is the repurposable resource hiding behind the product.

In this chapter, we'll look at how some companies like Amazon Web Services, Lotus Cars and LEGO have utilised hidden resources

> **Box 4.1**
>
> **Arm and Hammer and the multiple applications of $NaHCO_3$**
>
> Think about the many products Arm and Hammer has made based on sodium bicarbonate, $NaHCO_3$. To a scientist, $NaHCO_3$ is a molecule that has a certain nature. According to my friend Professor Karl Pestell, it's the amphoteric monosodium salt of carbonic acid, forming a white monoclinic crystal lattice at room temperature.
>
> To the purchasers of Arm and Hammer's products, however, it is variously baking soda, fridge deodoriser and even a home remedy for indigestion.
>
> It's baking soda because it foams during the baking process and so causes the dough to rise, fridge deodoriser because it is able to bind smelly molecules and a home remedy for indigestion because it neutralises acid which irritates the stomach. It has all these applications because of its nature. But thinking of it in terms of any one of its *purposes* is likely to block you from seeing the other applications. Who'd think of eating fridge deodoriser as a treatment for indigestion?

to create growth they hadn't even anticipated during their earlier business planning. We'll use a tool called the Hidden Resource Inventory to scan for hidden resources and clarify the platform for growth that you may already have but are overlooking.

The fundamental question is, 'Given all the things this business does, what foundation does it have for building things which are more distinctive, profitable, more popular, more efficient?' Influential management writer Adrian Slywotsky suggests distinguishing traditional accounting assets from what he calls 'entrepreneurial assets'. His question is, 'What do we have, *apart* from money, that an entrepreneur would love to have?' Some of these resources are obvious, but others are there as a side effect of the main purpose of the business.

For example, access to CEOs is invaluable if you want to test new value propositions. A start-up entrepreneur may be highly constrained because they just can't get that access. The risk for them is that however great their technology is, they end up building something superb but irrelevant. Conversely, if you are an established company, you might have access to CEOs who are otherwise protected by formidable gatekeepers, insights into consumer behaviour (because you're already in the market) or background IP – things you had to develop in order to put together previous products or services, but which are capable of being reused to get a new one off the ground more quickly.

Other potentially overlooked resources include data about customer behaviour and lessons you've learned solving your own problems that you can now sell to others.

Appreciating Your Most Valuable Resources

In order to appreciate your resources, it's necessary to be clear about what makes a resource valuable in the first place. It's worth spending a little time to consider this, so that as you apply the tools we'll meet later in the chapter, you have a better idea what you are looking for.

Valuable resources bring unique competitive advantages

Of course, business schools have looked at what makes business resources worth having. In fact the question is a cornerstone of the so-called 'Resource-based view of the firm'. Jay Barney's VRIO mnemonic will be familiar to anyone who's done an MBA. Barney asked the question, 'What has to be true for a resource to be a source of sustainable competitive advantage?' His answer was that the resource must be *Valuable, Rare, hard to Imitate*, and the company must be *Organised* to capture its potential value.

Barney makes it clear that it's not enough for a resource to be Valuable. At best, this will only give you competitive parity with others who can acquire the resource. Neither is it enough for the resource to be Rare. Crucially, unless it's also hard to Imitate, you'll get a temporary advantage at best while competitors figure out ways to get or build up the resource themselves. Ultimately, if your resource is valuable, rare, hard to imitate, then you've got a chance *as long as* you can also Organise yourself to exploit it. As Figure 4.1 shows, you can think of the VRIO criteria as a set of filters. Only the most consequential one or two resources will make it through the funnel.

A lot of managers want to keep their strategies a secret, but it's more powerful to make your strategy hard to copy. The ultimate strategy is one that is so difficult to copy that even though you can tell people all about it, they won't be able to copy you. Think of the companies that turn up in case study after case study: companies such as Apple, Southwest Airlines, IKEA, Zara and Netflix. Despite all the analysis of their strategies, these companies have managed to sustain their advantages over many years.

What makes you hard to imitate?

So what are the factors that make a business's strategy hard to imitate? Strategy theorists[2] have pointed out various factors:

- **Social complexity.** It's tempting to believe that businesses work the way it says on the organisational chart. But real organisations

Principle Two: Escape from Fixed Purposes

```
          Candidate resources
            ⬇   ⬇   ⬇
    ┌─────────────────────────┐
     \       Valuable        /
      \                     /
       \       Rare        /
        \                 /
         \ Hard to imitate/
          \              /
           \ Organised to/
            \ capture the/
             \  value   /
              _____/
                 ⬇
              Source of sustainable
              competitive advantage
```

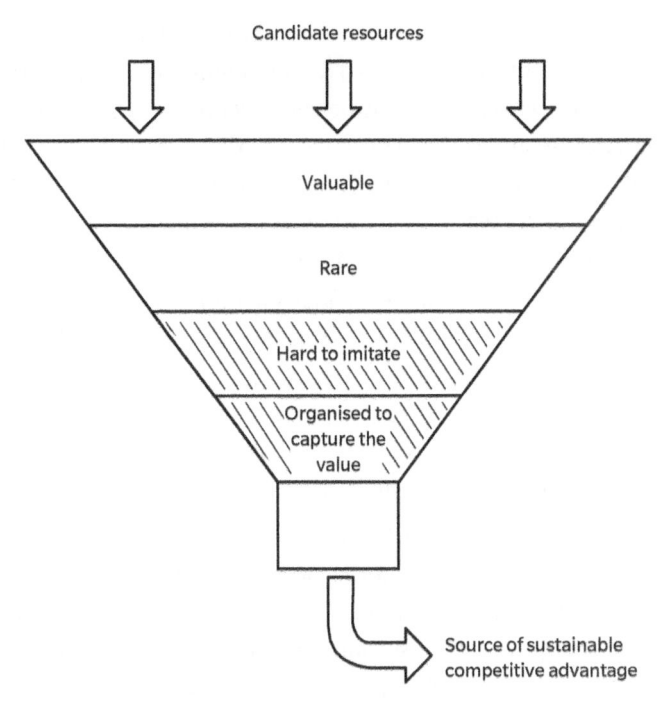

Figure 4.1 Based on Barney (1991). Starting with what works can lead you to your own inimitable advantages

have a lot of interconnections that are not on the chart. People build informal relationships in idiosyncratic ways: through conversations in cafeterias, in corridors, when commuting (and in the lockdown world, on Zoom). They tune in with some people, and get on less well with others. These webs of interaction can add a lot to an organisation – you learn who knows what, how to get things done by having a word with someone in accounts, or that an experienced engineer knows all about how to service old products. In successful companies, these relationships underpin trust, coordination and the spreading of useful knowledge.

- **Causal ambiguity.** Not everything that matters in an organisation can be documented. Neither can you codify every important skill. Steve Jobs famously once criticised Microsoft for 'having no taste'. Clearly taste is as an important factor in Apple's story. But how easily can you figure out how it works and emulate it?

- **Context.** Context really matters. I've talked already about the 'Rockstar hire' brought in from a famous company who disappoints in a new role. This person may be very talented, but the idea that their previous success is solely a result of their own talent could be way off the mark. More likely, their talent, plus the context of their old company – a great product, great admin support, a great team – all combined to produce their success.

- **History.** Uniqueness comes from idiosyncratic ways of doing things built up over years. The Toyota Production System was built up through millions of improvements over many years, underpinned by a particular culture. No one has been more written about than Toyota. Yet despite the extensive documentation, it has not always been so easy for would-be emulators to copy the results.

- **Trade-offs.** Even if a competitor can figure out what to do, it may be so costly to do so that they lose money trying. When the full-service airlines tried to beat Southwest at its own game, by creating their own low-cost solutions, they generally got into trouble because they couldn't copy the new strategy without messing up their existing commitments.

Valuable resources exercise
Part 1: Your most admired competitor

Get your team together to think deeply about your most admired competitor. Make sure you set aside some uninterrupted time. Start by explaining the VRIO criteria and ask your team to find examples from a range of well-known companies. Once everyone has got the idea, turn your attention to the competitor:

- What are their most valuable competitive resources? Don't just settle the obvious answers that first come to mind. Apply the VRIO criteria to test each possibility.

- What makes your competitor hard to copy? Is it social complexity? Ambiguous causes? A unique context or history?

- What would you have to trade off to reverse engineer them?
- How do they organise themselves to make best use of their VRIO resources?

Part 2: 'Red team' your own business

A red team is a group you convene to help you improve by playing the role of your competitor. The term originated in military training. Red teams can help challenge biased thinking, expose vulnerabilities and broaden conversations about strategy. Set up a red team to answer the above questions about *your* business's resources *from the point of view of your competitor.* How do you do? How can you strengthen your advantages and make them harder to copy?

How starting with what works makes you hard to copy

A business that copies others, and seeks saviour solutions from the outside, is unlikely to develop distinctive and hard-to-copy resources itself. On the other hand, by starting with what works, by modelling your own success, hunting out the underlying resources and bundling them in new ways, you naturally become more distinctive.

The Hunt for Resources: Three Levels

'What resources do you have?' is often too abstract a question to be useful. You can gather round a flipchart and have a brainstorming session to answer it, but in my experience people dry up fast. They just come up with a few obvious ideas no one can get excited about. I find that people need context, prompts and provocation.

In particular, it helps to think in terms of levels of granularity. As we discovered in Chapter 2, a key reason people find it hard to spot their reusable, repurposable resources is because they are looking at them at too macro a level. They need to appreciate more granularity. It's like the difference between the large DUPLO LEGO bricks, regular LEGO and then the advanced LEGO Technics that teenagers and adults like.

Big DUPLO bricks have limited possibilities, but they're a great place to start, and if they do the job, why make it more complicated? Regular LEGO affords many more possibilities, and LEGO Technics offers an incredible level of flexibility to build totally original designs.

- **Level 1: Generic resources.** At the first level of resources are generic business resources, such as capital, equipment and people. Of course you can ask yourself the question, 'How can we do more with these resources?' but it's pretty hard to come up with ingenious answers without more prompting. And any ideas you do come up with are likely to be cumbersome to do – those blocks are big, and it's major surgery to move them around. Venture capitalists have plenty of financial resources, but they have to get more granular than asking abstract questions like, 'What can we do with all this money?' Every once in a while they could luck out, but they generally get much further by finding start up entrepreneurs with well-developed ideas as to how to deploy that capital.

- **Level 2: Hidden resources.** The guiding question for identifying these is, 'What resources do we have that an entrepreneur would love?' These ideas are much more likely to tap into your uniqueness. It's a rich seam for investigation, and in order to help you find them, we'll look at some contemporary examples and prompts.

- **Level 3: Implied resources.** The third level is possibly the most exciting. These resources exist in the background. They can be discovered, not by looking straight for them, but by *inferring* their presence. These can be the most intriguing, and their effects the most transformational. They tend to be the most unique and inimitable too, since they are based on the idiosyncratic activities you've developed over time, shaped by your business's distinctive history of interaction with the outside world.

In the rest of this chapter, we will consider generic and, particularly, hidden resources. Implied resources will get a chapter of their own.

Level 1: Generic Resources

Figure 4.2 shows some of the generic resources any business will have. It also suggests companies whose generic resources might meet the VRIO criteria.

You can argue as to whether the resources given in these examples are really VRIO or not. It's certainly hard to find many examples of companies who compete solely on the basis of generic resources.

Furthermore, if you're looking for innovative platforms for growth, this DUPLO brick level of granularity might just be too macro. When you think at the low resolution of generic resources, you think about growth options in terms of enlarging a plant, buying more machinery, hiring additional staff and so on (in other words, expensive moves which lack ingenuity.) We need to zoom in further.

Resource category	Resource	VRIO example
Traditional Tangible Assets	Capital	J P Morgan
	Equipment	Shell
	People	Ideo
Traditional Intangible Assets	IP	ARM
	Content	Netflix
	Methods and competencies	Arup
	Brand	Coca-Cola

Figure 4.2 Generic resources

Level 2: Hidden Resources

As well as acquiring traditional resources like the ones we've just discussed, any established business will have developed 'hidden assets' without noticing it. You can often grow more quickly and easily by starting with these assets and connecting them to the emerging needs of your customers.

Remember, the guiding question here is: 'What assets beyond the traditional financial ones does my company own that an entrepreneur would love to have in order to create new value for customers?'

On Dragons' Den and Shark Tank, the best entrepreneurs often get multiple offers. It's not always the money that decides their ultimate choice. The smartest ones pick the Dragons and Sharks who can bring entrepreneurial as well as purely financial resources to the party.

As for well-established organisations, pretty much all of them will have built up entrepreneurial resources over time. Some companies recognise and exploit them brilliantly. For example, in Chapter 3, we saw how Cardinal Health was able to leverage its relationships with hospitals to get access to real surgical teams in action. That access is not something you can easily buy, however well funded you are. There are many other such examples: let's say you want to create a new fintech app. Wouldn't you love to have GoCompare's access to senior decision-makers at financial services companies, not to mention their data about how people buy financial services online?

Types of hidden resources

Let's look in more detail at the types of hidden resources that your company might have,[3] then I'll give you a tool to help you find them. Don't worry that some of these categories overlap. Some of the best resources could easily belong in more than one category. The most uniquely powerful might defy categorisation completely.

Relationship resources

Although they certainly receive attention, relationships remain some of the most under-exploited resources in many companies. People think of their value in a very linear way: they just see the straight line from a relationship to a sale. But your relationships provide all kinds of further growth possibilities, for example:

- **Customer interaction.** International Automotive Component Group's intensive interaction with car manufacturers allowed it to suggest innovative alternative interior panels that would enhance the value of a Ford model to *its* customers, the end consumer.

    Question to consider: Do we make the most of the opportunities to learn from and educate our customers during our interactions?

- **Reach.** Businesses as different as Tesco and Google can use their reach to bring new products to customers at scale.

    Question to consider: Does our reach to our customers and other contacts represent a unique asset we can capitalise on?

- **Alumni networks.** McKinsey nurtures its network of former consultants, many of whom become senior executives and then clients.

    Question to consider: Can we do more to leverage the value of our relationships with our former employees?

- **Insights into customer issues.** In the previous chapter we saw how Cardinal Health used their insights into surgical teams to produce procedure-specific kits. As another example, companies such as Siemens provide intensive data monitoring of their products in operation, to provide for predictive maintenance. The insights they get are invaluable for further innovation.

    Question to consider: What insights about our customers' businesses can we see that they may not?

Strategic position resources

Position in an industry can provide a great platform for growth. By dint of your position, you might enjoy access to information, negotiating leverage and new learning, as well as options to integrate forwards, backwards and sideways. For example:

- **Market position.** Somewhat controversially, accounting firms have built up huge consulting practices.

Question to consider: What needs arise for our customers before, during or after they interact with us? Can we advantageously meet those needs?

- **Access point.** Because of its role as an access point into insurance and related products, price comparison website GoCompare can partner with a wide range of financial service providers.

  Question to consider: Do we give advice to our customers about needs that we don't meet ourselves? Can we help directly, or as paid intermediaries?

Network resources

These clearly overlap with relationship resources. They are separated out here because the value is not so much in the individual relationship as in the multiplicative effect of the network.

- **Installed base.** HP printers are very reasonably priced, and of course that creates a huge installed based for selling printer cartridges. They've further extended the power of this model with HP Instant Ink, whereby they mail you replacement ink cartridges in return for recurring monthly payments.

  Question to consider: Do we have a customer base that requires ongoing help and supplies from us? Can we create car-wash style ongoing packages of support?

- **Third-party relationships.** Music tours are complicated things to organise. Tour management companies take the complications away, so artists can concentrate on performing. A crucial asset is their network of industry participants, including venues, technicians, professional service firms, travel and accommodation providers, logistic companies and so on.

  Question to consider: Do we know sufficient members of an industry ecosystem that we could act as integrators for our customers?

- **User community.** LEGO has cultivated its relationship with its vibrant adult user community to get feedback and even recruit winning designers.

    Question to consider: Do our customers know each other? Could we advantageously facilitate a community?
- **Ability to attract the right talent.** Google has no problem getting the best programmers. Fast-growing UK apparel company Gymshark is the place many of the young people I meet want to work. Both these companies have distinctive cultures that attract exactly the talent they need.

    Question to consider: Are we particularly attractive to the type of candidates we need? Are we a club that they want to get into?

Know-how resources

- **Systems and software.** Basecamp (formerly 37 Signals) initially developed its hugely successful project management software for its own use, then realised it had a winning product it could sell.

    Question to consider: Have we developed any particularly good in-house solutions (core, or non-core) that could be repackaged and sold?
- **Tech know-how.** Lotus Cars developed expertise in automotive suspension design through its long involvement in motorsport and high-performance car manufacture. It now consults on suspension design for other car manufacturers. Mercedes was able to respond to the COVID-19 crisis by turning its engineering expertise to the manufacture of ventilators.

    Question to consider: Where have we developed expertise that could serve other applications and new customers?

Data and information resources

- **Market Window.** ENSEK, fast-growing software provider to the UK energy sector, has a window onto the market which it can use to shape new products to meet emerging needs of its customers.

    Question to consider: What insights do we gain in the course of business that could have value if packaged for others?

- **By-product information.** The classic examples here are Facebook and Google, who, by gathering data as a side effect of facilitating social networking and search, completely upended the world of advertising. But these are just two of the most visible examples. Many companies collect huge amounts of data in the course of their day-to-day business – a trend that will only increase with the rollout of 5G networks. The information that is latent in that data represents a resource of rich potential for those who can organise and extract it.

    Question to consider: What do we learn by analysing data from our interactions with customers that could add value to them?

Reusable resources

- **Remanufacture.** The casings of gearboxes last longer than the cogs. In a classic example of 'circular economy' thinking, Renault adds new cogs to reconditioned old casings and sell the resulting product – highly profitably – at a discount.

    Question to consider: Is there exploitable value in our products after our customers have finished with them?

The ROI from hidden resources

Starting with existing hidden resources – instead of growing by enlarging a plant, buying more machinery, hiring additional staff and so on – can lead to:

- reduced development costs;
- accelerated time to market and ramp up of business;
- lower cost of customer acquisition.

So

- increased ROI on original investment in assets;
- better, faster returns from new business.

It also strengthens your unique resource base for the future. Finding and building on the hidden resources you've developed in the course of business is a great defence against reverse engineering, because it creates the causal ambiguity we discussed earlier. They can't copy you if they can't figure out how it's done.

Hidden resources inventory

Consider each of the categories, and ask yourself the prompting questions. Although some of the categories and examples will seem very different from the way you habitually think about your business, looking at your resources in new ways is the point. Therefore, it's a good idea to keep this question in mind: 'Am I absolutely certain this does not apply to me?'

Start with what works

Resource category	Resource type	Exemplar	Questions to consider	Example in your business
Relationship	Customer interaction	International Automotive Component Group	Do we make the most of the opportunities to learn from and educate our customers during our interactions?	
	Reach	Tesco	Does our reach to our customers and other contacts represent a unique asset we can capitalise on?	
	Alumni networks	McKinsey	Can we do more to leverage the value of our relationships with our former employees?	
	Insights into customer issues	GE	What insights about our customers' businesses can we see that they may not?	
Strategic position	Market position	Big Four Accountancy practices	What needs arise for our customers before, during or after they interact with us? Can we advantageously meet those needs?	
	Access point	GoCompare	Do we give advice to our customers about needs that we don't meet ourselves? Can we help directly, or as paid intermediaries?	

Principle Two: Escape from Fixed Purposes

Resource category	Resource type	Exemplar	Questions to consider	Example in your business
Network resources	Installed base	HP Instant Ink	Do we have a customer base that requires ongoing help and supplies from us? Can we create car-wash style ongoing packages of support?	
	Third-party relationships	Music tour management companies	Do we know sufficient members of an industry ecosystem that we could act as integrators for our customers?	
	User community	LEGO	Do our customers know each other? Could we advantageously facilitate a community?	
	Ability to attract the right talent	Google, Gymshark	Are we particularly attractive to the type of candidates we need? Are we a club that they want to get into?	
Know How resources	Systems and software	Basecamp project management	Have we developed any particularly good in-house solutions (core or non-core) that could be repackaged and sold?	
	Tech know-how	Lotus Cars	Where have we developed expertise that could serve other applications and new customers?	

Resource category	Resource type	Exemplar	Questions to consider	Example in your business
Data and information	Market window	ENSEK	What insights do we gain in the course of business that could have value if packaged for others?	
	By-product of interaction	Apple iPhone sleep app	What do we learn by analysing data from our interactions with customers that could add value to them?	
Circular economy	Remanufacture	Renault	Is there exploitable value in our products after our customers have finished with them?	

Principle Two: Escape from Fixed Purposes

Exercise
Key hidden resources

Look at the resources you have identified above. What new applications do they suggest?

	Resource	VRIO score*	Possible new application(s)	Value to customer
1				
2				
3				

*(V = 1, VR = 2, VRI = 3, VRIO = 4)

Where Next? Implied Resources: A Preview

As you work to more deeply appreciate the resources you have already, you are searching for elements to recombine in new ways to create greater value. While generic resources can be found on the balance sheet, and hidden resources are often hiding in plain sight, there's a third level: what I call 'implied resources.' In the hunt for implied resources we look at what is already working and ask, 'What must be there in order for this to work, and what else can we do with it?' This is where your truly unique assets might be lurking, and it's the subject of the next chapter. Read on to find out more.

Chapter 5

Principle Three: Reverse Engineer Yourself

'Discovery is seeing what everybody else has seen, and thinking what nobody else has thought.'

Albert Szent-Györgyi

Chapter 4 was about starting to realise the abundance of resources any company has acquired without noticing it. We did this by providing examples and prompts, and in particular by contrasting the conventional balance sheet view of resources with the entrepreneurial view. Starting this way builds confidence and can spark inspiration.

In this chapter, we'll be drilling deeper into the details of your own unique vault of what I call your *implied* resources. An implied resource is something that logically must be there for the things you do to work. I find that people often overlook or discount these resources. Building off your implied resources can lead to growth options that are:

- more original;
- harder to copy;
- potentially easier and cheaper to implement (because you're already doing some of what's required).

GoCo Gets Granular

GoCo owns GoCompare, one of the UK's leading financial product price comparison websites. Founded as an insurance comparison site in 2006, the business expanded by adding naturally adjacent categories such as energy, loans and broadband.

But it has gone much further than that, partly because it had to. Its competitors had built up similar positions and it was hard for customers to tell the difference. As CEO Matthew Crummack explained to me, 'The comparison site market had got to the point where everyone thought that success was only ever about whose TV advert people would remember: our opera singer vs the competition's furry animals.'

Matthew and his team saw that view as extremely limiting. After all, the hassles customers have in navigating the opaque financial services market are confusing and costly. The potential solutions are sophisticated and can bring them a lot of extra value.

One of those solutions is auto-switching, which GoCo added through the development of WeFlip and the acquisition of Look After My Bills. Since then GoCo has continued its development using the kind of approach we'll focus on in this chapter.

Sorting through its resources, the GoCo team recognised the opportunity to bundle them up into an architecture they call SaveStack. SaveStack consists of a collection of elements each providing a 'microservice'. Each does a single useful job to help customers manage household finances. So there are microservices for payments, for switching suppliers, for shopping and so on. These elements talk to each other to provide various tailored solutions to the customer.

The fascinating thing is that this quickly became more than an elegant approach to software engineering. Why? Well, the more the team followed the SaveStack approach, the more innovative possibilities it gave them.

For example, they realised they could take the same microservices they used internally, package them appropriately, and offer them to external partners. So now, Virgin Bank uses the capabilities of SaveStack to enable its bank account customers to switch energy suppliers. From the customer point of view, this is all part of a seamless experience within their Virgin account.

SaveStack is an example of a granular 'LEGO Technic' way to do more with what you already have working. Let's look more closely at that approach.

Level 3: Implied Resources

The scanning tools we used in the previous chapter are based on *analogy*: I've given you some examples and suggested you see if you can find something similar. This can be very effective, but it does tend to lock people into fixed categories of thinking. It can be hard to escape from those categories. Especially if you're thinking in large LEGO block terms, the possibilities for reconfiguring things are limited.

So in this chapter we go more granular. The idea is to look at the specific things that work in your business directly, without likening them to other examples, and to reverse engineer the results-producing mechanisms you have. This is where you're most likely to find unique and hard-to-copy ideas.

Start with what works

How programmers constantly reuse stuff that already works

Some of the most powerful insights about reusability come from computer programming. These insights apply more widely than just to writing apps. I first came across them in my undergraduate days as a computer science student. But it's not necessary to understand all the inner workings of computers: the principle I want to share is quite intuitive.

One of the most important lessons a new programmer learns is that if you organise things right, you can reuse the same bits of computer code to do lots of different – but related – jobs for you. Here are a couple of examples:

- If you've written some lines of code that will draw a table of five columns and ten rows, you can easily make a more general version that will draw *any* number of columns and rows that you ask it to.
- Or, a bit trickier, if you come up with something that will sort a list of *names* into *alphabetical* order, you can use the same basic procedure (the 'algorithm') to sort a list of *dates* into *numerical* order. The pattern is the same, even if the data and context change.

Creating a general 'tabulator' or a 'sorter' has lots of advantages. The most obvious one is that once you've got something working, you can reuse it in new situations, and you'll have saved lots of time.

During the early stages of learning to program, a lot of what you are learning is to spot opportunities to reuse code this way. You start by generalising code to cover different but obviously related problems. The real art is to transfer code between jobs that don't necessarily look related.

You don't need to know the details of how to code to grasp the idea. For example, let's say you start with the code to draw a 5 cm circle across in the centre of the screen.

Principle Three: Reverse Engineer Yourself

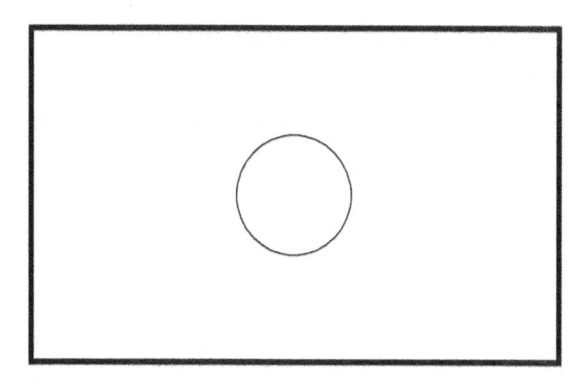

The next step in learning to program might be to generalise that code so that it could draw a circle of *any* size in the centre of the screen.

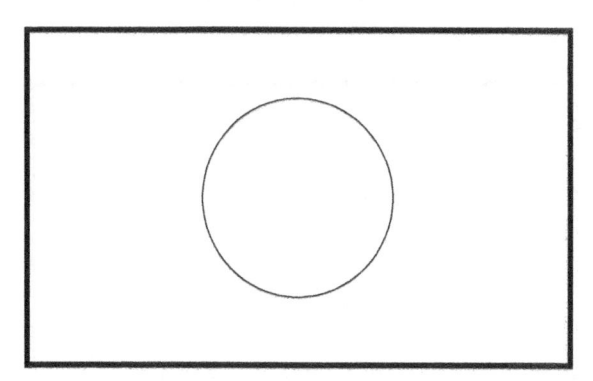

Then you could generalise it further to draw a circle of any size, in any *position* on the screen.

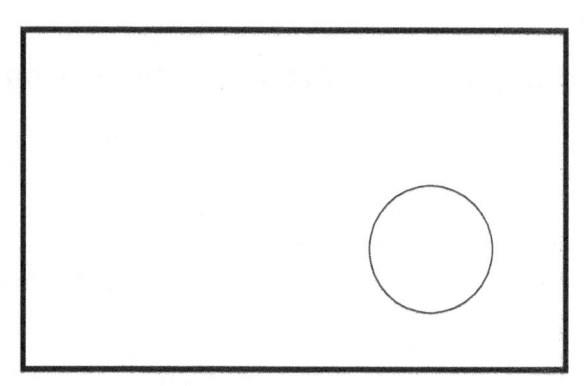

Then you could repeat the pattern twice, centred on two points, to draw a Venn diagram.

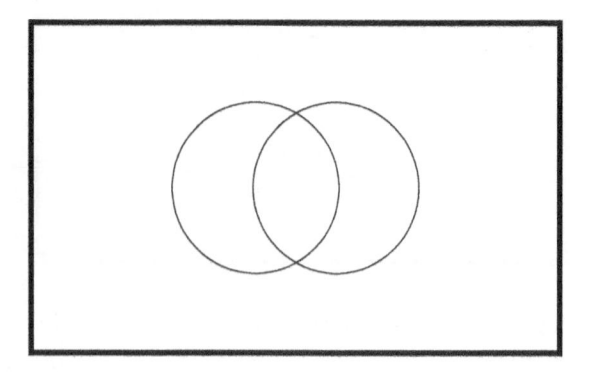

You could even repeat a few more times, with two sizes, so as to draw the Olympic rings.

And so on.

Reverse engineering what's already working

This is where things get interesting. Once you get the idea of generalising code, you can work in the opposite direction. Any experienced programmer can interact with a piece of software and figure out what *must* be there in order for it to happen, at least in outline. In other words you can reverse engineer your way back to identify the implicit resources!

So if you saw a program that drew Olympic rings, you could make some inferences; for example,

1 it must contain the code necessary to draw a circle in different positions;
2 it must be able to repeat the same operation a number of times, varying some parameters as it goes;
3 if it can do that, it must therefore also be possible to draw *other things too*, say, the Audi logo:

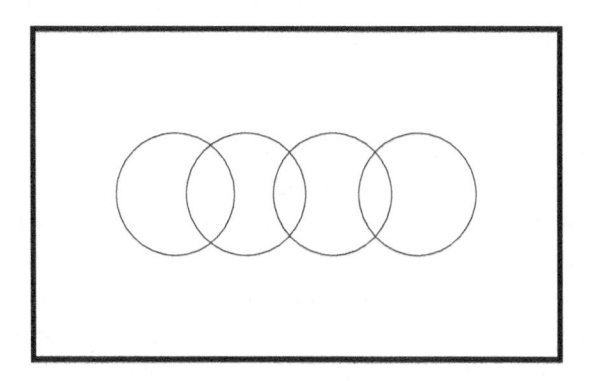

Going further, we can infer other resources and possibilities. For example, the code must be relying on the ability to light up any specified pixel, and therefore could draw other shapes you might want.

How does this apply to the hunt for resources?

In our hunt for resources, we can look at things that are working in the business and infer what *must be there* that we might be able to apply elsewhere. This is what I was driving at with the discussion of GoCo. GoCo didn't start out providing software services to banks, but it noticed that if it packaged up the microservices it relied on in the right way, a new growth opportunity opened up.

Or consider this example in a very different sector. McDonald's doesn't seem to be a property company, but that's how Ray Kroc characterised it in a discussion with University of Texas MBA students.

Maybe it's best to see the twenty-first century McDonalds as *both* a property company and an operating company. The operating company has rediscovered a number of times in its history the value of staying close to its core: burgers. What about the property company? One of its implicit resources is great expertise in footfall analysis, vital for selecting prime sites for new restaurants. Could that form the basis of a consulting offering to other retailers or even to town planners? Note that I'm not saying that they *should* to this, that's a strategic choice dependent on many other factors. But for our purposes, it makes a good illustration of this chapter's theme of reverse engineering yourself.

To keep things tidy, you can use a table like Figure 5.1 to describe an implicit resource, ways of packaging it, and the value for that for clients.

How might these value-producing elements look in a Car Wash framework? Have a look at Figure 5.2.

This is just a thought experiment, but I think it's possible to imagine such a consultancy offer being attractive. We've already seen that Lotus Cars makes around half its revenue from engineering consultancy based on know-how it built up in racing and sports car design, and Unipart – originally a car parts supplier – built a profitable consulting arm focusing on sales and factory improvement.

The value of looking for implied resources

To succeed in a competitive business, you have to offer customers a clear and different choice. If you are the same as everyone else,

Implicit resource	Package	Value for client
Ability to predict best location for retail outlets based on modelling foot fall and flows through urban locations	• Consulting for retailers in different industries • Consulting for town planners	• Increased revenues • Better urban environment

Figure 5.1 Implicit resource table

Element / Bundle	Footfall analysis and site selection	Then how about: Business case development	What else? For example, acquisition strategy advisory	What else?	What else?	Value
What else?						
What else?						
Gold	*	*	*			
Silver	*	*				
Bronze	*					

Figure 5.2 Fictional MacDonald's consulting Car Wash options

customers will just choose whoever is cheapest or most convenient. But being different feels risky. There will be many voices in favour of the safe, the proven, the 'industry best practice'. These voices often discount the risk of being indistinguishable from competitors. Starting with what works, and particularly starting by leveraging your implied resources, offers a way out of the dilemma. The more you build off things you are already doing uniquely well, the more chance of distinguishing yourself at acceptable risk.

How to Look for Implied Capabilities and Resources

1. Ask: 'How do we 'do' our product?'

Think back to the computer programming metaphor. The essential point is that any specific behaviour implies a more general capability.

- Pick a product to look at.
- What are the procedures implied by doing it successfully? Are any done particularly well?
- What resources must be there for this to work?
- What else could you do with those procedures and resources?

2. Ask: "How do we 'do' our business, and how else can we use that?"

Look now at the wider set of activities in your business.

- Look at the details of the various things that happen in your business. For example:
    - delivering things;
    - financing things;

- inventing things;
- maintaining things;
- supporting things;
- selling things.
- What has to be working for these things to happen successfully?
- What are the implied resources?
- What else can be done with them?

> **Box 5.1**
>
> **Ocado: From grocer to global technology provider**
>
> Ocado, founded as a British online supermarket, never operated retail stores, choosing instead to deliver direct to customers' homes. As Ocado grew, it developed the hardware and software to support its operations. Only later it realised that this infrastructure was a huge asset and packaged it up in the shape of the Ocado Smart Platform. Through this platform, Ocado serves supermarkets across the world, including Morrisons (UK), Group Casino (France) and Kroger (USA). Reconfiguring from UK grocer into a global technology provider has given Ocado dramatic growth prospects.

3. Look for excellence outside your core areas

In case the first two methods are too analytic for your tastes, try this approach suggested by Rooney Anand, former CEO of Greene King plc (and now Chairman of WorldSkills UK). Look for corporate old wives' tales and trusted mechanisms that are *not* part of the core overt business, yet are key to success. It could be for example the way your business forecasts, buys, tests, sells or solves problems. You're looking for areas that haven't changed over the years. Not because of inertia, but because they are really good, often because they were developed by a real enthusiast.

Examples that are non-core:

- large management consultancies need to be good schedulers;
- a company might be particularly effective at navigating its customers' accounts payable departments in order to get paid and could provide that as a service to others.

The natural point of focus in a business is on the core elements. After all, these are seen as the ones that maximise value to the client or customer; they're obvious. People often think of old processes as the domain of middle management, and as a place where problems and waste reside. This is axiomatic in the once-popular idea of 'reengineering the corporation'. But sometimes, the opposite can be true.

I remember hearing an interview with Jonathan Miller, the polymath doctor, computer researcher and theatre director. He was asked what the most important innovation in medicine had been in the twentieth century. His answer was a surprise: not penicillin, or better anaesthetics or better surgical techniques, but 'better nursing'. Now, you can certainly make an argument that instead it should have been the other things, but this shows Miller's sparkling intelligence and his ability to think more contextually.

Similarly, look at Formula One. The emphasis tends to be on the drivers and the car designer. But what about the pit crew? Their supporting role in the sport itself has been much appreciated of course, but their skills have also enabled F1 teams to consult on the organisation of surgical teams. Pit crews have learned a lot about extremely lean, error-free and fast coordination through the arms race in pitstops, and this know-how turns out to have valuable application in other areas.

The trend towards outsourcing and shared service centres has often positioned non-core activities as the Cinderella parts of the business. Yet is that the best way to look at it? The logic of outsourcing is that other people can do it better than you. But that's not always the case. And if *you're* better, maybe you can become a value creator for someone else.

4. Stand an old cliché on its head

An old cliché for creativity is to ask, 'How many uses can you find for a brick?' The brick question is actually a good exercise, although you are more likely to find distinctive applications if you identify an implied resource and then ask, 'How many uses can you find for *that*?' So for example, 'how many uses can you find for huge experience of footfall analysis in urban areas?'

There's some really interesting psychology here. In their book *Inside the Box*, Boyd and Goldenberg report research by Fiske.[1] People are much more able to answer questions of the form 'What other problems can you solve with *this*?' than they are answering questions of the form 'How many ways can you think of to solve this problem?'

We are actually more ingenious and prolific when we answer the first question than the second, and historians of invention think that more progress has resulted from the former.

5. Explore the significance of anomalies

One of the best places to search for implied resources is in the exceptions to day-to-day performance. Performance in businesses is rarely evenly distributed. But the tendency of management reports is to average things out, meaning they can hide important factors (recall that old joke about a statistician who drowned crossing a river of an average depth of two feet).

Whatever your average performance, it's likely some of your interactions with the world have standout levels of performance. They are too often discounted as anomalies.

Elite organisations and top performers are much more acutely attuned to positive anomalies. They are also more appreciative of the significance of things. For example, the MIT first-year programming course described the course like this:

> 'By learning to program you will acquire one of the most significant and powerful problem-solving processes known to humankind.'

Most course descriptions would have said: 'Programming is a well-paid job' or something similarly mundane.

So how do you sensitise yourself to positive anomalies? You can use both formal and informal ways of going about it. You could do some complex analysis of quantitative measures, but you can also do it qualitatively by being alert to surprises.

For example, call centres are notoriously bad at customer service, so when they've been good, I have on occasion asked to speak to the operator's supervisor. The operator is usually crestfallen until I reassure them, thinking I'm about to complain. The supervisor is even more surprised. After the call, I always wonder if they will take the opportunity to figure out what that operator is doing well and to spread that internal best practice around the call centre?

Systematic things to do

- **Practice 'de-averaging'.** Look beyond the averages to see, for example, which specific customers are the most profitable or the most satisfied. Where are operations particularly efficient? Ask: 'What accounts for the differences between the exceptional and the average?' Richard Koch, author of *The 80/20 Principle*, has made a whole investing career out of this approach.[2] Yet where he recognised its significance, I've heard others discount the approach with an off-hand, 'Oh it's just the old Pareto effect'.

- **Notice surprise testimonials.** If a customer is particularly pleased, do you hear about it? Are you putting things in place to find surprise testimonials? Would you be notified if one came in? As well as complaints procedures, you need to make it easy for you to be notified when things are going well.

- **Don't *just* give recognition.** Many businesses have Employee of the Month, or Plant of the Year awards. If these high performers genuinely stand out, it's worth figuring out their recipes so you can mine them for further applications.

6. When is a by-product not a by-product?

There's often an emphasis on the negative by-products of processes – for example the NOx emission created by internal combustion engines. But sometimes by-products can be incredibly positive.

Consider this: Michael Smets, Professor of Management at Saïd Business School at Oxford University, drew my attention to the fascinating example of chickpea water, or Aquafaba. Aquafaba is the viscous water resulting when chickpeas are cooked. It turns out to have application as a vegan egg white substitute that can be used both at home and in the mass production of vegan food products including meringues and marshmallows.

7. Flip your mental frame with scaling: Ask, 'How come we aren't worse?'

I was in a first meeting with the operations director of a shopping centre. We talked about how things were going in general, and the director happened to mention a recent employee satisfaction survey that had produced very disappointing results. Actually he confided, the management team felt pretty demoralised about it. Clearly the poor feedback needed to be addressed. But to do that effectively, we had to do something about management morale so they could engage with the issue with positive expectations. Currently their opinion of the business was being framed by the survey results. To help connect the director with the resources he had available, I had to rebalance his mental framing of the situation.

I said:

'Well, despite the disappointment of that survey, we have other information. As you'd expect, I did a Google search before coming here today. I believe you have 50,000 visitors a day. That's up 7% on last year. Somehow, the vast majority of those visits go smoothly. People do their shopping, eat and use the various facilities. Some of them temporarily lose their kids and are reunited with them by your staff. There are first-aid incidents that are handled without drama. I've visited as a "civilian" many times myself, and know from my own experience that when a friend of mine lost their phone in a cafe, your staff handled it with cheer and reassurance. They found the phone for him and seemed delighted to have helped. So I know that at least some of your staff members have pride in their work. I also know that I personally have never had a bad experience in many visits. And come to think of it, I've never heard anyone else complain either. So, although this is all anecdotal, and although you've clearly got an issue to address here, you must be doing some things right. In fact, a load of people must be doing a load of things right. If we were to work together, that's what I'd want to start with.'

The director's mood visibly brightened, and at the end of the meeting, he said to me: 'Your comment completely transformed my perception of how we're doing. I feel a hundred times better.' As you can imagine, we started working together soon after.

Even an average performer is doing lots right. We don't tend to focus on that. Here's a brilliant technique – called Scaling – for flipping people's mindsets. It's a technique from the world of solution-focused therapy that has also proven its worth in business.

Here are the steps.

1 In relation to your current situation, (whether you think you've got a problem or are taking proactive steps to grow), ask yourself: 'What's my best hope?'
2 Create a scale. If your best hope is 10/10, and its opposite – whatever that means to you – is zero, then where are you on the scale?
3 Most people say something in the range of 3 to 7. Let's say you pick 5.
4 Then ask the question: Why aren't we a 4? What is stopping us being *worse*? We must be doing some things right.

5 Inventory the reasons you are at least a 4. What are those strengths and capabilities? What's working? This is what I did informally with the shopping centre director. Be exhaustive in your search for these positive reasons (the question I use to drive my clients mad here is 'What else? What else?')

6 Then look at those strengths and capabilities and ask yourself what you can do with them.

We'll revisit this scaling idea with a new twist in the Epilogue: 'You go first.'

8. Recognise your survival and resilience resources

This approach is based on the following premise: to survive, you must have dealt with various challenges. To do that, you must have drawn on effective resources. There are basically three ways to handle survival challenges.

1 **Buffering.** This is the approach of the boxer – you build up fitness and strength in order to survive external punishment without internal damage. It's probably indispensable, and it certainly works up to a point, though it won't stop you from getting bloody. In business terms, this might mean having strong enough reserves of one sort or another: the obvious generic example is a strong financial position, but it could also include having great security arrangements, enforceable patents and strong litigation. Any and all of these could be reusable resources.

2 **Building your agility so you can neutralise the widest range of unbufferable disturbances.** Taking hits is hardly an adequate defense on its own. This second approach is like the aikido strategy of being able to flow with and around attacks or shocks. In business this is about having decision-making sufficiently close to customers and suppliers – for example, the ability to resolve customer problems elegantly, instead of using PR to limit the damage (which is more akin to having a good cornerman in the

boxing example). Where can you find great examples of internal best practices of agility?

3 **Building up your antifragility.** Nassim Taleb coined this concept in his book, *Antifragile*.[3] He asked, 'What's the opposite to fragility?' Most people answer with words like robustness. But he points out that if fragile things are broken down by stresses, shouldn't the opposite be things that are *strengthened* by stresses – like muscle tissue for example? Looking at it this way, muscle is antifragile (it's not a coincidence that Taleb is a keen dead lifter). Where has your organisation learned from shocks? This is certainly a viable path into interesting consulting offerings. For example, De Becker and Associates is a world leader in celebrity protection. Their capabilities are based in no small part on behavioural insights and skills Gavin De Becker acquired during a dangerous childhood.

Where have your company's responses to challenges – for example, the recent COVID-19 crisis – left you stronger, so that you can teach, consult, invent, or otherwise transfer those resources to new situations?

A Reinvention Thought Experiment: Giving 'Sin Stocks' a Way Out

> *'Always give your enemy a way out.*
> *If you totally surround them, they will fight even more fiercely.*
> *With a way out, they will not.'*
>
> —Sun Tzu, *The Art of War*

This final example pushes the idea of using implicit resources by applying it to a very hard situation: reinventing a company facing an existential threat.

With the rise of Socially Responsible Investing (SRI) and the Environmental, Social and Corporate Governance (ESG) agenda more generally, there are many industries which are experiencing pressures from governments, health organisations, campaign groups and even shareholders. What is the future for companies with questionable ethics?

Some will no doubt attempt to 'fight even more fiercely.' But others might be open to change if they could see an escape route. However, even if they want to unwind their activities, it may be very difficult, in no small part because of many people whose economic futures depend on their continued existence. Take the tobacco industry, for example. As badly as individual growers have sometimes been treated, they still depend on cigarette manufacturers for their livelihoods. And many otherwise innocent pensioners may also depend on the preservation of value in these companies.

Let's say a cigarette company decides to get out of tobacco completely. And they don't want to cram into the overcrowded temporary life raft of vaping, judging it economically shaky, and no more than a moral half-way house unlikely to satisfy dissenting stakeholders.

What do they do? Well, what if they start by looking for what works – what are cigarette manufacturers good at? They certainly used to be world leading in sales and marketing – in the history of advertising it's hard to think of a more iconic image than The Marlboro Man. But governments have severely limited what cigarette companies can say and do over the last few decades. Marketing is unlikely to be a strong suit now. They need to look somewhere else.

How about procurement and logistics? Buying is extremely challenging: how do you maintain consistency with all the agricultural variables at play? And what about the capability to distribute to hundreds of thousands (millions?) of locations globally, often in places with challenging infrastructure?

What have cigarette companies had to learn in order to do that? What are the underlying routines, know-how and relationships? And: what else could these things be used for?

For example, how might those provide support for online e-commerce distribution? Or medical distribution? What about synchronising large networks of small producers of other crops, such as sorghum? (Sorghum is increasingly in demand. It's used for food, in sorghum syrup or 'sorghum molasses', as animal fodder, in the production of alcoholic beverages, and in biofuels.) In case this thought experiment seems fanciful, did you know that Coca-Cola, a business with comparable abilities to get their product to far-flung locations, uses this capability to distribute medicines in their existing boxes? They pack them in the spaces between the necks of the bottles.

An ethically questionable business is unlikely to unwind its harmful activities without an economic path for it to do so. Starting with what works may be its best chance of a way out.

Summing Up: Will a Great Idea Work in Practice?

In my experience, teams find the process of uncovering new ways they might use overlooked resources – whether generic, hidden or implicit – extremely energising. It's great to come up with new ideas like this, but just because they are based on what is already working doesn't mean that they will work themselves. So, in the next chapter, we'll bring some scientific humility to temper any alchemical hubris, and *let the world teach us what works*.

Chapter 6

Principle Four: Let the World Teach You

> 'Nature, to be commanded, must be obeyed'
>
> Francis Bacon (1620), Novum Organum Scientiarum ('New Instrument of the Sciences')

In the previous three chapters we looked at various ways to break down what we already have and build up again into new ideas for growth. The more you find this hidden gold, the more you will see a wide range of overlooked growth possibilities for your business. As we said in Chapter 1 though, the ability to identify potential is only half the equation – to benefit, you need to bring that potential to fruition.

It's one thing to come up with new possibilities. It's another to know whether any of those possibilities will succeed or not. Even expert financiers and CEOs get predictions wrong, and market research can be dangerously misleading, because customers are not good at predicting their own future behaviour.

People launch initiatives based on wishful thinking, dubious assumptions, sycophantic market research responses, or the highest paid person's opinion. In their enthusiasm they build the wrong thing, they spend cash on the wrong thing.

Finance people are well aware of this. They attempt to manage the risk through elaborate business planning templates. But these introduce their own problems:

- Some people get very good at gaming the process – often lobbying the organisation's influencers – and get poor ideas funded.
- People who are sure that an idea is bad stop things that actually could have been breakthroughs.

The problem in both cases is misplaced certainty. It's better to have the attitude of celebrated screenwriter William Goldman: 'Nobody knows anything . . . Not one person in the entire motion picture field knows for a certainty what's going to work. Every time out it's a guess and, if you're lucky, an educated one.'[1]

It's not just true in the movie industry.

So it's best to treat even the most promising-seeming idea as an educated guess, as a hypothesis to test, preferably as early and inexpensively as possible, and before seeking massive injections of new resource.

Whatever the highest paid person in the room says, and whatever the marketing research suggests, the world is the ultimate arbiter of what works. In these fast-moving times, beware of grand plans laden with unwarranted assumptions. Even plans resting on highly plausible analysis regularly turn out to be ungrounded. Pursuing such plans wastes a lot of resources.

Yet if you ask the world the right way, it will teach you what works, giving you a confident basis for scaling things up. So use what you already have to test your assumptions before you waste money. This chapter will show you how, like Zappos and others using disciplined experimentation, you can identify the key assumptions which could sink a business idea and test them in the real world as early and cheaply as possible.

Find Out What Works in the Real World Before You Waste Money

In around 2000, when investors were falling over themselves to get in on the dotcom boom, a startup called Webvan raised hundreds of millions of dollars to build an online groceries business. Advised by their backers – experienced Silicon Valley venture capitalists – to grab first-mover advantage, they built a state-of-the-art distribution centre, complete with automated picking system, and bought a fleet of distinctly shaped delivery vans to emphasise the brand in consumers' minds.

Unfortunately, they selected the wrong market, and revenue never caught up with investment. It's not that they neglected market research. Let's be clear that the Webvan team, like their investors, was a group of clever and successful people who acted on the basis of careful business planning. They had research showing that their offering was a service with mass appeal. But while market research respondents said they liked the idea of home delivery, the reality was that they wouldn't actually pay for it when the time came.

Contrast this with the approach taken in the early days of Zappos, the online shoe store now owned by Amazon. As Eric Ries explains in his book *The Lean Startup*, the founders of Zappos did not spend much money to start with. They built a simple website and populated it with photos of shoes taken at a local shoe shop. If a customer placed an order online, someone from Zappos went down to the shoe shop, bought the shoes, and delivered them to the customer personally. The Zappos team verified the key assumption that *people would buy shoes before trying them on.* If that assumption turned out to be false, there would be no business. However, once they knew that was true, they could think about other aspects required in order to grow.

How Much Can We Learn from Past Experience?

I once wrote an article in which I extolled the way UK supermarket giant Tesco scoped out the US market when planning the launch of their Fresh & Easy stores. I talked about the fact that they had executives hang out with families and learn the way Americans wanted to shop – a way which is quite different from customers in the UK due to the layout of shopping areas and freeways, work and domestic routines and so on. Anyway, as valid the 'see the world from the customer's point of view' message remains, Tesco's in-depth research wasn't enough to do the trick on its own. Fresh & Easy struggled and Tesco pulled out in 2013. There appear to be a number of reasons: US consumers were already spoiled for choice, the name Fresh & Easy reminded some shoppers of a deodorant rather than a grocery store, the company didn't embrace coupons, which British shoppers are unenthusiastic about, but which in the US are something of a national pastime. None of this invalidated the point I was making, but it certainly took the shine off my example. So, although I don't do much futurism, one prediction I feel safe in making is that I will do less of it in the years to come.

It's fun to look back at predictions made by pundits and business leaders. For example:

- In 1977, Ken Olsen, founder of Digital Equipment Corporation, said, 'There is no reason anyone would want a computer in their home.' (Olsen had at that point built DEC from a garage start-up to be the second biggest computer manufacturer in the world – we can suppose he knew a thing or two about the computer industry.)

- Darryl Zanuck, a producer at 20th Century Fox, said in 1946 that television wouldn't last because, 'people will soon get tired of staring at a plywood box every night.'
- In a 1995 Newsweek column, astronomer Clifford Stol said 'no online database will replace your daily newspaper, no CD-ROM can take the place of a competent teacher and no computer network will change the way government works.'
- In 2007, Steve Ballmer, then CEO of Microsoft, said, 'There's no chance that the iPhone is going to get any significant market share. No chance.'

Clearly being successful and clever says little about one's prediction abilities. Even one of the best, most sensible and innovative writers on strategic management, Henry Mintzberg, got caught out:

> 'Enron,[2] with its "loose-tight" management policy, is an example of an organisation that has figured out how to effect change without the usual pitfalls', says Mintzberg. 'The Houston-based energy company manages only two corporate processes very tightly: performance evaluation and risk management.'[3]

Mintzberg is indisputably top-drawer – so when I read how wrong he'd been about Enron, I didn't feel quite so bad about my Tesco blooper!

Are there any lessons here? Well, for would-be pundits: 'Don't make sweeping predictions', obviously! But more seriously, how about the following?

- Don't be too quick to emulate the 'best practices' of an apparently successful business venture.
- Don't mistake over-confident extrapolations from a 'model' or set of beliefs for what is developing in the real world.
- Do think twice before writing off the competitive threat of new ideas or substitute products which would threaten your currently successfully, even dominant, business model.

- Do either base the business on human needs which don't change much or make sure you have an agile organisation: one which can perceive and respond to threats to the assumptions that got you where you are today.

You know when someone comes up with a business idea and asks what you think of it? It's a tricky moment, because your answer will necessarily be an opinion. Remembering the advice of screenwriter William Goldman, when it comes to the question of whether a new idea will work, it's safer to assume that, 'No one knows anything'.

Then what can be done?

When you give or seek an opinion on a business idea, it's best to treat that opinion as an educated guess. If you want to sound sophisticated, you can call it a hypothesis.

And what are we supposed to do with hypotheses? We're supposed to test them with experiments (and if we are going to manage risk, we're going to do the test as early and inexpensively as possible).

Remember the Segway – that two-wheel personal transporter in the film 'Mall Cop'? There were plenty of opinions about that one. A lot of people thought the Segway was going to be a massive hit. They thought it was cool. Not many ever bought one, though.

If the developers of the Segway had tested the assumption that people wanted another alternative to the many existing modes of personal transport, they may have got an unpleasant awakening. But they would have also saved millions of dollars which they could have used to pursue something else with their talents. Similarly, if Steve Ballmer's Microsoft had taken an iPhone to the trading floor of a bank, they might have discovered that BlackBerry fans would be happy to trade in their keyboards for a touchscreen.

'That's all fine for you to say in hindsight,' you might reasonably challenge. 'But what can I do in advance?'

Answers from Silicon Valley – often filed under 'Lean Startup' or 'Customer Development' and basically boiling down to applying the scientific method to business innovation – have jumped from start-ups to older established organisations such as GE and Intuit, often with great success.

In outline the process goes like this:

1 Identify the key assumptions underpinning the business idea.
2 Find the riskiest assumption – treat it as a hypothesis.
3 Design the cheapest and quickest experiment you can to test the hypothesis.
4 Use what you learn to accelerate, modify, or if necessary, drop the idea.
5 Rinse and repeat.

Testing a business idea in this scientific way takes guts, especially when the evidence might threaten our precious idea or the boss's idea. But the transition from superstition to science has always taken courage, and all innovation has depended on it.

Box 6.1
A hard train to stop

Ranjit Das of the Hunter Centre for Entrepreneurship at Strathclyde Business School is a former GE FastWorks coach who worked with Lean Startup originator Eric Ries. Ranjit was based in GE's Oil and Gas business. He made the following observations:

Getting funding for a project in most businesses is a difficult process. A major problem is when you need a lot of money. People want reassurances. You have to jump through many hoops, and fill in many forms and spreadsheets. You have to show very attractive ('hockey stick') growth based on guesses and the unreliable say-so of potential customers. You also have to lobby senior finance executives to give your idea their stamp of approval. The danger now is that the executive has invested not only money but their personal prestige in the project.

> What happens then, when you reach a stage gate in the process and the project is not on track? As Ranjit points out, 'It's a hard train to stop.'
>
> The point about lean startup is not that it improves your hit rate of ideas – it probably doesn't. What it does is much better steward your development funds. Instead of saying, 'Here's $10 million over the next two years to work on this product', you're saying, 'Here's $50,000 over the next 6 weeks to test the first make-or-break assumption. If it turns out to be true, we'll give you some more to move to the next step. If it turns out to be false, we can discuss a pivot, or we'll agree to pull the idea (saving $9,950,000 and 98 weeks that we can all use on something else). In essence, let's find out what works before we put all our money into it.

Learning from the Lean Startup

There are a number of descriptions of the Lean Startup process, including Eric Ries's original Build-Measure-Learn loop, but the one I find clients grasp most quickly is the one that appears in Figure 6.1, which Ranjit Das introduced me to on a project we did together.

Understand customer needs and identify candidate offerings

I've grouped these two together, because they're not as sequential as the diagram – and a lot of 'rational' development processes – might suggest. Sure, sometimes you start with a clearly articulated need from a customer for which you then go away and design a neat solution. And occasionally someone invents a totally new technology and it finds a ready market.

But more often, you pick up a vaguely articulated dissatisfaction from customers, or on the other hand, you may have an idea which

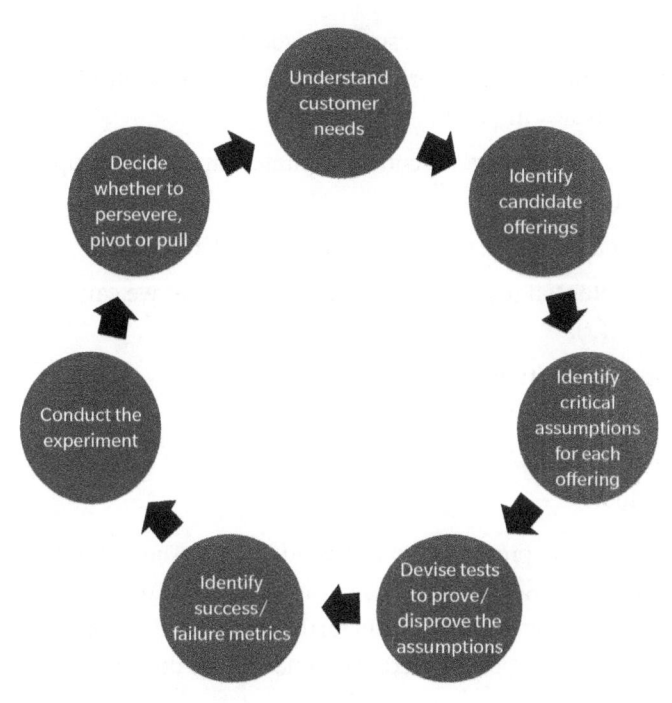

Figure 6.1 A Lean Startup loop (adapted from Ranjit Das, used with permission)

has potential but isn't yet packaged up so that customers can recognise its value. This is likely true of ideas developed by looking for hidden resources and bundling them into potential offerings. That's why we then need to move to the next step of identifying the crucial assumptions.

Identify crucial assumptions

The critical or leap of faith assumptions are those things which a business idea rests upon. They are the things that must be true if the idea is to work, for example:

- What people are prepared to do (e.g. we'd beable to get service staff to initiate sales conversations.).
- What resources you would need access to (e.g. we'd need to persuade supermarkets to give us shelf space).

- Competitor actions (e.g. customers would prefer our offering so much that a competitor couldn't win them away just by undercutting our price).
- Supplier actions (e.g. we could guarantee an adequate supply of needed materials).
- Sales potential (e.g. there are sufficient buyers for this).
- Profit potential (e.g. if we can generate the sales we can turn it into profit).
- Cost of acquisition (e.g. we can acquire customers at a cost that leaves us some profit).
- Growth potential (e.g. there are affordable ways to reach new customers).

There's no way to prove that you've listed all the assumptions on which an idea depends. So it makes sense to apply a variety of methods to come up with a list, to go back and forth between the methods, and to involve a variety of people. Here are some ways to do that.

a. Tap into your intuitions and experience, and those of your team.

Simply ask yourselves: 'What has to be true in order for this idea to work?'

So in the case of the Zappos, example answers include:

- People have got to be prepared to buy shoes without having tried them on.
- They have to be willing to risk the hassle of returning the shoes.
- They have to believe they will get a refund.
- The shoe shop will have to have the shoes in stock when we want to buy them.

b. Use standard business model frameworks as prompts

There are a range of frameworks based on past experience and analysis of the elements that businesses need to have. You can use these as templates: your best guess about the answer for each element becomes your hypothesis. For example, all business models need to identify as a minimum a value proposition, a method of sale, target customer segments, payment structures, key activities, a method of distribution and a financial model. Different templates tend to emphasise a different views of business, so it can make sense to use more than one. If you need more detail, you can consult one of the popular frameworks, such as the Business Model Canvas, The Lean Canvas, Strategy Maps or Driving Forces.[4]

c. Tap into the power of your naysayers

This is a great opportunity to use a resource that you may not appreciate: the naysayers in your business. You know who I mean: those frustrating people who say 'No' to every idea. Here's where they can add a lot of value.

You can ask them: 'What would cause this idea to fail?' And they'll tell you. Then, you can flip their list of objections into your list of hypotheses. So if you ask, 'What would stop this working?' and they say, with all the charm you have come to expect, 'This is a stupid idea, because no one will order shoes they haven't tried on', then your hypothesis becomes: 'People will order shoes they haven't tried on.'

Rank assumptions in the best order to test them

Figure 6.2 shows a convenient chart for ranking your assumptions so that you test them in the most efficient order.

Design economical experiments to test the assumptions

In Lean Startup jargon, the way you test an assumption is by building a Minimum Viable Product or MVP (think of Zappos' combination of a simple website, local shoe shop and a team member to buy and deliver the shoes). As often happens with jargon that catches on, MVP is now a phrase that's used to refer to all kinds of ideas beyond its original scope.

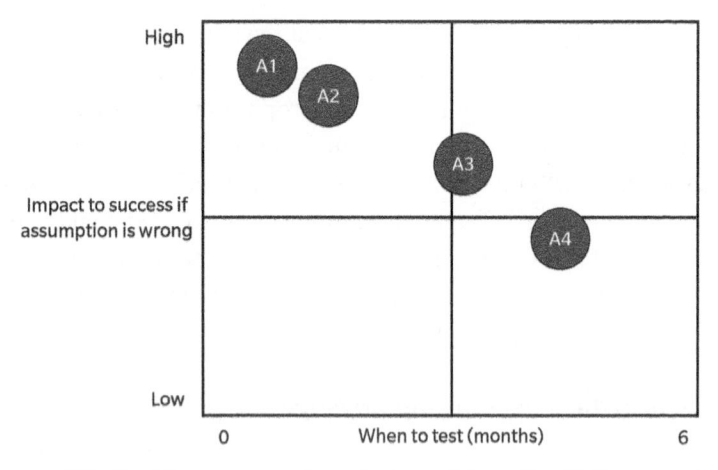

Figure 6.2 Ranking assumptions (adapted from Ranjit Das, used with permission)

Talking about MVPs rather than simply 'experiments' risks a number of misunderstandings about what it takes to test an assumption:

- *Misunderstanding #1: You need a complete product.* Minimum viable *product* puts a particular picture into people's heads. Some hypotheses can be tested without having to build any kind of 'product.' For example, you might be able to test someone's willingness to buy with a simple PowerPoint presentation followed by a request to sign a letter of agreement. Building any kind of product before testing that willingness would just waste time and money.

- *Misunderstanding #2: Minimal means shoddy.* No, the experience of the customer should be good. From the customer point of view, the early Zappos experience was a good one. The fact that it was implemented by 'a man behind the curtain' didn't detract from the value they received. If you build a shoddy product, however, it will distort your feedback and potentially damage your reputation by disappointing the customer.

- *Misunderstanding #3: An MVP is a prototype.* Not necessarily. 'Prototype' implies a pretty complete solution. The danger is that in designing and building a prototype, you'll again spend time and money on aspects unnecessary to test the hypothesis.

- *Misunderstanding #4: It's a pilot.* No. People promise their backers a pilot to show they are managing risk. But pilots are often designed to 'prove' what the person has already decided. The pilot is a bit of theatre. At best you learn a few things so that you can tweak the subsequent main project, but it's rarer that a pilot leads to cancellation of a project, or a substantial pivot. One healthcare executive told me that when they'd tried to implement lean startup, one team had tried to game the whole process, staging fake experiments, feeding in bits and pieces of 'evidence' but always intending to implement their preferred idea, because they were sure they were right about it.

So, for all these reasons, it's better to keep things jargon-free and just talk about experiments. Then you can ask simply, 'What's the *least* we'd need to do – ideally using what we have already – to show that the assumptions on which this idea depends are false?'

In this connection, I am sometimes amazed at how people casually add unnecessary cost and complexity. One business wanted to test the assumption that existing customers would be prepared to be upsold to a new (Car Wash style) 'Option 2' bundle. They planned to fly to a customer's location to show a mocked-up brochure and ask for a letter of agreement that if the product was implemented, they would buy it.

I said, 'Could you do this over Skype instead of flying to see them?'

They replied, 'Well it's better to see them in person.'

I tried again. 'Well let me ask it this way: 'Can you disprove your idea over Skype?''

'Yes,' they conceded, and we instantly saved €3000 and two days.[5]

Conduct the experiment and use the results to decide your next step

If your experiment works, you can move on to test your next hypothesis, and once you've checked them all, you can proceed to scaling your idea.

If, however, your experiment fails to work, you have two options.

1 You can modify your idea, taking into account what you have learned. This is the famous 'pivot', another term that is now highly overused but in this original sense is very useful. A famous example of a successful pivot is provided by PayPal, originally an electronic wallet for use on Personal Digital Assistants (PDAs), until its value as a secure payment method for eBay was recognised.

2 Stop the train. Stop pursuing the idea, and redeploy your resources on something else. Notice how much easier it is to do this if you framed the exercise as a low-budget experiment rather than the first step in an expensive, high-stakes project.

Making sense of 'failing fast'

'It doesn't matter how beautiful your theory is, it doesn't matter how smart you are.

If it doesn't agree with experiment, it's wrong.'

– Richard P. Feynman,
Joint winner of the Nobel Prize in Physics, 1965

Webvan's founders and investors were undoubtedly smart people, with solid track records and a beautiful business plan. So, most likely, were the executives who refused to 'stop the train' in light of evidence suggesting projects they'd approved were coming off the rails. The point is that once you've gone to all the trouble to start a big project, it's hard to stop it.

One of the great values of this experimental approach is that it reframes 'failure' into 'learning.' Sure it might still be disappointing if an idea turns out not to work, but it's not the threat to the ego, or perceived threat to careers, that a failed product might be.

Talk of innovation often engenders fear. Leaders will say things like 'We need to fail fast', and 'If you want to increase your success rate, you need to increase your failure rate'. It sounds good, but unless you have the structures, it's a tough ask. Few people are sufficiently stoic. Indeed hearing such slogans, many employees will do a quick mental calculation and decide, 'Interesting, but better to concentrate on safe bets' – these are the people who are answering 'Yes' when asked to innovate, but are then rationalising their lack of progress by saying, 'I was busy with the day job.'

Adopting the experimental mindset really helps. After all, if an 'unsuccessful' experiment quickly saves the company from wasting money pursuing a dead end and instead points it in the right direction, it's an extremely valuable thing.

Paying Attention to What Actually Happens

It's now well known in the start-up world that a new venture can have too many resources, and therefore end up wasting them. Better to start small and experiment in order to understand what you've got before you ramp up the investment. As we've seen in this chapter, you can't start with what works unless you know what works. And to find out what works you have to pay attention to what actually happens. Let's now look at that in more detail.

Chapter 7

Principle Five: Watch What Actually Happens

Customers are often unable to articulate their needs or predict their buying behaviour in imagined scenarios – a fact that limits the value of traditional market research. We saw this in the previous chapter in the case of Webvan, where respondents declared themselves enthusiastic about ordering groceries online, then failed to follow through.

When Disney launched their stores, they built a realistic mock-up on a spare movie lot, invited people in, and watched what actually happened. This unfiltered approach – using existing resources to explore a possible new future – provided much better information than externally commissioned interview responses. Marriott followed a similar path in developing their time-share villas, achieving higher revenues from smaller spaces than predicted. You can similarly find or set up situations to discover valuable insights from what actually happens (and GlaxoSmithKline are now working with Birmingham City University to learn similar lessons using Augmented Reality).

Behaviour Is the Best Information

Disney stores are like catnip to kids. I remember visiting a shopping centre with my then four-year-old niece. As we reached the bottom of the escalator, we were faced with the racy shop front of Ann Summers, the lingerie and adult products chain, complete with under-dressed mannequins in the window.

'Uh oh – hope she doesn't ask about this,' I thought.

I needn't have worried. Because next door was The Disney Store. My niece locked on to it like a heat-seeking missile, oblivious to the adult-oriented window display right in front of her.

How do Disney stores achieve this effect? They didn't figure it out by asking young children what they wanted – after all, the kids were unlikely to be able to articulate it. Instead, at the advice of board member Steve Jobs, they built a Disney Store on a movie lot, and observed kids while experimenting with the design and layout, gauging improvements by watching what achieved the most animated responses. They realised that the best information was behaviour, not words.

Focus more on what people do, less on what they say

Adult customers are often no better than kids at articulating their needs or predicting their buying behaviour in hypothetical future scenarios. (Rory Sutherland, Vice-Chairman of leading advertising and marketing agency Ogilvy UK and author of *Alchemy*, remarked to me that a lot of market research is pretty misleading for this reason.)

Before you think that this is just other, crazy people, let me ask a question: have you ever said one thing, and then done another? Of course! Everyone has at one time or another. One trade association I worked with habitually surveyed its members about what to include in its events programme. Members would clearly prioritise lectures and educational site visits over social gatherings. That makes sense – such events have more career value, and the members were ambitious. It's amusing, however, that the turnout was always much better for the summer barbeque!

People are not good at predicting what they will do in hypothetical situations. And that goes for customers, employees, suppliers and peers. It's rarely mendacious, but it's what actually happens. Yet when businesses gather information, they often carry on as if words always equal deeds – very much to their cost.

It's not that they're lying . . .

Children learn early in life – perhaps they simply stumble upon it – that one option open to them is to say things for effect rather than to convey truth. In the film *The Invention of Lying*, Ricky Gervais's character reaches a similar conclusion. We can create effects that are useful to us and that could not have been achieved otherwise.

Out-and-out lying is one thing. A more perplexing issue for researchers is when 'saying-one-thing-and-doing-another' arises out of a desire to be polite, or to please, or avoid offending a questioner. And often, respondents genuinely believe that their intention is to do the thing they said, but then their minds or circumstances change, and they do something else.

So, reserving the term 'lying' for deliberate attempts to mislead, and deferring discussions of moral grey areas, it's important to recognise saying-one-thing-and-doing-another as a ubiquitous fact of human social life.

Well-designed psychology experiments take care to factor such biases out. It's tricky. In fact even when asked an anonymous question on a self-completed survey, or online, people may provide an answer that reflects their preferred self-image rather than how they will behave in the actual situation. The trade association members' real preferences for barbeque – in contradiction of their worthy-sounding questionnaire responses – provides an amusing but telling example.

What does this mean for your business? Well, when a survey or focus group respondent is asked a question about likely purchasing behaviour, or how they will respond to a change in terms and conditions, how do you know you are getting good information? And, if you are conducting an appraisal with a direct report, in which you have influence over their compensation, ditto? Could this be adversely affecting the information you're using for your decision-making about customers and employees? You bet.

The best guide to what people do is what people do, and that is often very different from what they say they will do.

Don't *just* listen to customers

So while 'Listen to customers' is good advice, it's not the full story.

To start with though, what is the good part of this advice? Well, it's easy for businesses to get a bit arrogant and think they know better than customers. Assuming that they know better than the customer is a problem, especially for businesses based on sophisticated expertise – like vehicle manufacturers, law firms, consumer electronics companies and software houses.

It therefore seems to make sense to listen to customers but why is that not the full story then? Because, as Henry Ford is supposed to have put it: 'If I'd asked customers what they wanted, they'd have said: "A faster horse"'.

Think about it as a customer yourself. Haven't you ever rejected the idea of a new product or service you now can't live without? Did you know you wanted an iPad before you'd ever seen one? I remember for years how many people would pooh-pooh the idea of having a mobile phone!

Customers have only a partial insight into what they want, and their answers to questions about it are unreliable.

So if you can't depend on your own opinion of what customers ought to want, and if you can't trust what they say, where can you get some dependable information? You have to pay attention to what customers actually do. This of course is a crucial design factor for the experiments we discussed in the previous chapter.

Four ways to focus on what customers actually do

1 **Make sure your experiments require *skin in the game*.** In the previous chapter we looked at using experiments to test business hypotheses. Here's an important refinement. It's not enough to show a minimum viable product (MVP) and ask, 'Would you buy this?'. You need to ask for an action that costs the other person something: perhaps money, or a commitment to spend money, or their time, or their prestige. For example, when GE were exploring the idea of a stripped-down ultrasound scanner for use in China, they asked doctors, 'Would you be willing to write to your hospital administrator (thereby putting some prestige at risk) recommending that if we build this scanner, the hospital should buy it?'. If a prospective customer is willing to put some skin in the game, they are actually doing something, not just saying that they will.

2 **Build mock-ups.** We saw how Disney built a realistic mock-up of a store on a movie lot then observed how children behaved in response to various tweaks in configuration. In the early 2000s, Marriott decided to build more TimeShare villas at their Shadow Ridge resort in Palm Desert. They wanted to build villas that were smaller than the existing design, but somehow make them feel more desirable. Chairman Bill Marriott had a few different designs built as free-standing mock-ups. These were located directly behind the sales office. When potential customers came to consider a purchase, rather than show them the existing units, sales staff took them to one of the mock-ups to gauge their responses. Over a period of 18–24 months Marriott continually re-designed the mock-ups based on customer feedback. They eventually homed in on a design with a 10% smaller footprint, that nonetheless attracted customers willing to pay more than the rate for the older, larger units.

3. **Take your mock-ups into the virtual world.** GlaxoSmithKline (GSK) Consumer Healthcare has brought the idea of watching what actually happens right up to the minute. Their Shopper Science Lab (SSL) investigates how shoppers make decisions and what influences their choices. Like Disney and Marriott, the SSL uses mock-ups that look like a real shop, supermarket or pharmacy. Where it goes further is in the use of digital technology to support its research. For example, GSK sends consumers on 'shopper missions' and use tools such as mobile eye tracking to analyse their behaviour. They can then use the data as interview prompts, leading to deeper insights about the consumers' decisions. Working with Birmingham City University's Digital Media Technology Lab, GSK is now extending the approach to use Augmented Reality. They are building virtual shopping environments and products, enabling them to more quickly and flexibly test new ideas.

4. **Observe people in the current surroundings.** You don't always need a mock-up, of course. Huge amounts of useful information about customers and employees go unattended in the daily stream of activity. Executives are easily cut off from this stream, spending so much of their time in meetings, on Zoom calls, and reading reports and spreadsheets. This factor is so important that it's worth a section of its own.

Stuck in a Reality Bubble

Two young fish are out for a swim. An older fish is coming upstream and asks cheerily: 'Morning kids – how's the water?' One young fish turns to the other and remarks: 'What the hell is water?'

The water is so taken for granted that the fish are totally unaware of it.

A fool's paradise

At a UK division of a European manufacturing firm, I heard the MD claim that above and beyond their engineering excellence, their key strength, the factor that really set them apart was the quality of their service. This was accompanied by nods of self-satisfied agreement from his team and the representative from the parent company. When you spoke to customers however, they told you that the service department was arrogant and unresponsive, and expected customers to fit in with their procedures and to do so on the company's timetable.

Clearly the MD wasn't talking to customers, and was just believing the convenient stories told to him by his sales and services staff.

Why aren't more executives curious about what it's like to be their customer?

Remember the film *Stepford Wives?* (coincidentally written by William Goldman, whose admonishment that no one can predict hit movies we discussed in the previous chapter). The film features a young woman who begins to suspect that the wooden-acting housewives in her new neighbourhood are robots programmed by their husbands. It turns out this kind of programming doesn't just happen in the movies. It goes on all the time in call centres.

I once found a mysterious large withdrawal on my bank statement. Attempting to preserve a veneer of calm, I asked the 'personal banker' at the call centre to tell me where my money had gone. She replied in a sing-song voice, 'I'm sorry it doesn't tell me.' I asked her to check again, and after a delay, got the same result. I began to feel a rising sense of panic. After a pause, she cheerfully continued, 'Is there anything else I can help you with today?'

. . . Anything ELSE?!

Taken aback, I managed a distracted 'uh, I don't think so . . . ', to which she quickly responded, robotically following the script, but still Stepford-cheerful: 'Thank you for calling ABC Bank.'

Thankfully, the money magically reappeared in my account later that day; I never had any explanation beyond, 'It was just a mistake'. Whenever I have recounted the story, there have been nods, wry laughs and winces of recognition, followed by 'I-can-top-that tales' in return.

So much for one of the worst customer experiences of my life – what's it like *working* in such an environment? I'm going to guess that the Stepford Personal Banker started that job as an intelligent, articulate person who understood the importance of serving the customer. But the company has trained her – in fact forced her – to behave stupidly, at least while at work. All she does all day is to follow the script offered up on her computer screen. The screen tells her how to respond. It makes the decisions. And as long as she eventually gets to say, 'Is there anything else I can help you with today?' and receives the answer 'No', that counts as success, regardless of the actual situation in which she has left the caller.

It must be demoralising for the employee, which means a further degradation of the customer's experience too.

Do senior leaders ever call their own inbound call centres? The cheapest, easiest and arguably best information a leader can get is available by shopping at their own business. A surprising number show a remarkable lack of curiosity about what it's like to be a customer, or indeed a customer-service employee.

A submarine without a periscope

The French High Command at the start of WW2 – at the Château de Vincennes, in Paris – was described by one staff officer as 'a submarine without a periscope'. The resulting lack of awareness did nothing to help their ability to cope with the Blitzkrieg from the East.

As it is for Generals, so it is for business leaders. Executives risk living in a world mediated by memos. They easily end up talking only to direct reports, the board, investors and advisors. Without noticing it, they quickly get cut off from reality.

- One MD was shocked to read in a trade magazine that his number one competitor had been awarded a contract he hadn't even known was available to bid on. This was a substantial company – with an excellent reputation for its engineering – in a B2B market where just 10–20 contracts were available per year.

- Another CEO had been begging his engineers to build a slimmer version of a ventilation unit used in commercial buildings, only to be assured that the physics meant it was impossible. Imagine his surprise when he finally left his office and went to a trade show, to find the competition displaying a 'physically impossible' slim ventilator. He kicked his display stand over in anger in full view of the trade show delegates. You can imagine his horror and embarrassment. The competitor was out with the product now. How long would it take to work out what they were doing and get something into production? And, even more worrying, just how far behind the competition were they? (You could fairly ask in response to this example: 'What do you do if your own experts tell you something is impossible? Ronald Reagan put it best: 'Trust, and verify.' If the supposedly impossible would be truly transformative, or if customers keep asking for it, you owe it to yourself to check with relevant academics or consulting engineers.)

- So often I find – and, ominously, I've heard turnaround professionals say the same – that answers to serious challenges to a business are likely to be found in the heads of frontline staff, customers or even people like trade journalists – but they have never been asked.

There is no need to seek deep psychological explanations for all this. We can readily observe the human tendency to cut ourselves off from reality, even when the stakes are as high as they could be.

Get out of the corner office and see for yourself

I remember one CEO telling me that his big worry was isolation. Not emotional isolation, but isolation from real information. He felt stuck at the end of a corridor, in a corner office, and found it very hard to really know what was going on in his company, with his customers, or indeed in the wider world. He seemed to see the board and his investors more than anyone else. All information came to him in the form of reports. His diary was scheduled for him, and access to him was strictly controlled, albeit with the best of intentions. If he ventured out of his office into the corridor, the people he met were highly motivated to reinforce his existing view of the world.

'And I'm supposed to be in charge here!' he half-joked.

He was a particularly intelligent, insightful and personable guy. This was not the result of wilful neglect or a tendency to complacency. It had crept up on him.

To solve the issue, we put together a list of new people and places to visit, and new experiences to seek out, and off he went on tour. He visited designers, academics (and not just business school academics), advertising executives, TED talkers, computer geeks, and so on.

He came back with fresh perspectives, renewed energy, new ideas for the business and new ways to inspire and lead his people. And he started having fun at work again.

All of us – and not just CEOs – can get sealed up in our own reality bubbles. It takes active work to resist, and it gets worse – and the isolation gets more dangerous – as the pace of technological change accelerates.

Seven things to do to break out of a reality bubble

Different tactics make sense according to the nature of your business, so choose whichever of these make most sense in your situation.

1. Call your own call centre, or visit your own website, to get a quote, make a return, or make a complaint.[1]
2. Like Lord Sieff, the legendary chairman of M&S in its heyday, visit one of your locations *incognito*. (Lord Sieff used to dress as a tramp to see whether he would be treated with compassion.)
3. Shop at your competitors. When Alan Mulally was CEO of Ford, he and his executive team used to drive either a current Ford model or a competitor's to work every day.

4 Work a shift. Especially a night shift, since people are used to far less management presence and so you may get some interesting surprises (and it has the added bonus of demonstrating more effort and commitment than if you turn up during the day).

5 Visit universities who are researching technologies relevant to your business, or any technologies that are being hyped in the press. They will generally be delighted to talk to you and may be able to cost-effectively help with R&D questions.

6 Spend time chatting with a diverse range of interns and placement students – you can often get more insights about consumer behaviour that way than by hiring consultants to do focus groups, plus you'll learn about what they consider to be cool technology and social media trends.

7 Participate in peer roundtables with leaders from unrelated industries.

When You Notice What Works, Call for More of It

Years ago I attended a coaching skills course that ran over a number of weekends. One of my fellow participants, call him John, was a football coach at Nottingham Forest's Academy. John was very experienced at coaching up-and-coming footballers, and was looking to transfer his skills into performance coaching for business. His own son was an apprentice at Bolton Wanderers Football Club and played matches most Sundays, so I got to overhear John and his son's post-match phone calls. It was fascinating to hear the way John handled these calls. He wasn't particularly concerned with the result of the match (who cares if Bolton Wanderers' apprentices beat Stoke City's?). What he wanted to do was maximise his son's chances of becoming a professional – that was the goal. To him, the apprentice matches were essentially experiments. In analysing those experiments, John always asked his son three questions: 'What did you do right?', 'What did you do better than last time?' and 'What are you going to do next?' He directed his son to attend very specifically to what was working and to plan to do more of it next time out.

Contrast this approach with what typically passes for 'feedback.' Usually it's nothing more than opinion, which creates unreality and even dependence. A typical exchange might go as follows:

Manager: 'That was a great presentation.'

Staff member: 'Thank you.'

The manager walks away congratulating themselves on offering praise. But, did the staff member really learn anything they could use to improve?

And consider those 'feedback forms' that ask you to do the following sorts of things:

How would you rate Mary's work attitude?	1 2 3 4 5
How would you rate the content of the session?	1 2 3 4 5
How did we do?	1 2 3 4 5

What is anyone supposed to do with the number? How can the recipient adjust their actions in order to improve?

What feedback really is, and what it is not

Feedback is *steering information*, not opinions, evaluations or judgments. Think of a sailor with their hand on the tiller, maintaining course by keeping the mast aligned with a star. The ship is constantly being diverted by the wind and the waves. The visual gap that opens up between the mast and the star is information fed back to the sailor, who continuously acts to close the gap. It's this feedback process that makes successful navigation possible.

Heinz von Foerster[2] defined feedback as 'The return of part of a system's output to change its input'. In other words when the star drifts to the left relative to the mast, that is feedback that the oar is too much to the right. The sailor can recognise his behaviour (the way he is holding the tiller) and its effect in the world (the drifting of the star to the left) and adjust accordingly.

The Captain could stand by the sailor all night saying, 'That's good', or 'That's bad', or 'I rate you as a 6/10 steersman', but it wouldn't help performance one iota. The performer must recognise their own behaviour and its effect in the world.

Let's return to the manager giving feedback to the presenter. As we said, to tell the presenter 'You gave a very good presentation' doesn't tell her much she can use. On the other hand, what if you provide feedback in terms of what actually happened? For example:

> 'You started with an intriguing and relevant story, and when you did, people started to lean in and follow you. They sat back and paid less attention to that slide with all the bullet points though. You summarised your message succinctly at the end, which generated animated discussion and a clear decision.'

Now the presenter has steering information. The manager – acting as a coach – has drawn her attention to what worked, reinforcing it for the future. The presenter also has clear ideas as to how to build further on what's working.

Directing attention to what actually happened is the royal road to powerful feedback and accelerated performance improvement. That performance can be individual, as in the case of the presenter above, or organisational. Saying, 'The kids loved the Disney store mock-up' is nice, but it doesn't tell you what to keep and what to tweak.

The three feedback questions

Here are those three questions I learned from John, the football coach:

1 What did I (or we, or you) do that worked?
2 What worked better than last time?
3 What do I want to work on next?

Notice how the first two questions direct attention to what actually happened. They are deceptively simple, so I hope you will take them seriously enough to try them. They work amazingly well both to tell your mind to continue to focus on what is working and to frame disappointing results in as constructive a light as possible. (The real accelerator question is number 2, because it encourages more of what is working – literally a 'runaway success'.)

The three feedback questions are great to ask reactively after a key performance: a presentation, a sales call or an innovation experiment, for example. It can be even more powerful to ask them proactively at the end of the day, week, month and year, to create an ongoing process of evolution and growth.

The exercise in Figure 7.1 combines these timeframes and is something I like to do periodically with my coaching and mentoring clients.

You can easily see how to use this framework with others. Try it today: pick three people and tell them what they are doing that is working, what they are doing that is improving, and suggest what to work on next. The three feedback questions give you a simple, quick and pragmatic way to create improvement by starting with what works.

The power of noticing what's actually happening

I was in Amsterdam for a meeting with colleagues about the role of design thinking in innovation. I returned to the UK via the city's Schiphol airport.

	... today?	this last week?	... this last month?	... this last year
1. What worked ...				
	Since yesterday?	Since last week?	Since last month?	Since last year?
2. What improved ...				
	Next?	Over the next week?	Over the next month?	Over the next year?
3. What would be most profitable to work on ...				

Figure 7.1 Three feedback questions over four timeframes

Keen to eat before the flight, I was disappointed to see long queues at Passport Control. I looked past the crowd of forty-or-so people to see if I could estimate the waiting time. Passport control was fully automated: three gates, each with a passport scanner, a camera and an automatic barrier. Most people were coping with the scanners, but it still looked like I was going to be cooling my heels for a while.

Then I noticed something unexpected. Although there were three gates, there were only two lines. Nobody was waiting for gate two. I wondered if the machine was broken. From a distance it looked okay. It showed the same green lights as the other two machines. But maybe I was missing something.

I walked hesitantly between the two long queues of people. I felt sure I was about to be stopped by somebody for pushing in, but no one said a word. I approached the machine, intently looking for an indication that it was out of service. But no, it seemed fine.

I put my passport in the scanner. A few lights flickered, but the barrier remained closed. 'Uh, oh,' I thought, 'It will be embarrassing if it turns out I missed a big sign that said this lane is out of service.'

But then the barrier swung open! I went to look for a restaurant, chuckling to myself while the people behind me continued to wait. Some were probably unaware that lane two was empty. They were on autopilot.

Maybe some were jet-lagged. However, I think a larger number of people saw and considered the empty lane, but talked themselves out of investigating. They decided that because no one else was using the lane, there must be some hidden problem. Despite the evidence of their own senses, they weren't about to risk looking foolish to find out if the opportunity was real.

Businesses, of course, do the same. They play safe and copy each other, and they pay the price as their strategies converge. That's why so many offerings – cars, supermarkets, phones – seem the same, and why competing businesses subject their customers to the same annoying automated messages ('Unexpected item in bagging area,' 'Your call is important to us').

It's how unimaginative price wars start. And it's how big opportunities are missed or taken. Remember when you used to have to carry your heavy suitcase through the airport? How many luggage manufacturers thought of putting wheels on suitcases, but didn't follow through? (Bernard Sadow got a patent on a wheeled suitcase as recently in the history of the world as 1972, and incredible as it seems now, there was a lot of resistance to the idea to start with). It takes confidence in your own senses – and the willingness to test what they seem to be telling you – when the crowd is doing something else.

'But that's where the opportunities are,' I reminded myself, as I parked my rolling suitcase in the airport restaurant and grabbed the menu.

Of course it's one thing to attend to what actually happens. A second question is, 'Which of those things actually matter?' Let's turn to that question in the next chapter.

Chapter 8

Principle Six: Find the Few Things That Really Make a Difference

The worst kind of waste is doing something that doesn't make a difference to your audience, customers or employees, and doing it really well. Experts can easily fall into this trap. Engineers build products and design services based on their own view of what is required and end up adding features the customer doesn't appreciate. Organisational development consultants run elaborate training workshops full of material that's never applied. The antidote is to ask: 'Where are we working hard on things that don't make much difference?'

It's in the Hands, Not the Bat

Manchester YMCA, 1955. The table tennis club had four tables. Beginners started at Table Four. If you won, you moved up. At Table One, the winner stayed on. The standard at Table One was high – those players were junior championship contenders: young, fit, serious about their equipment, dressed in immaculate whites. If you fancied your chances, you were welcome to have a go. Most likely you'd hardly even see the ball.

So one afternoon this old guy (he must have been at least forty!) wandered in. He was wearing long trousers, a shirt and tie – and braces! He didn't even have tennis shoes – just worn brogues. He raised eyebrows when he joined the queue for the top table, then triggered smirks when he asked to borrow a bat.

The Junior National Champion had been on since lunch and had dispatched all comers. The old guy wiped the floor with the young champion, and stayed on the table for an hour or so as others tried their luck. Then he checked his watch, thanked the fellow who'd lent him the bat and ambled towards to door.

'What just happened?' asked one of the young blades.

Their coach, who had slipped in unnoticed half an hour earlier, had been watching with amusement. 'Oh Mr Miller used to play for England. I guess it's in the hands, not the bat.'

Some Things Make All the Difference, and a Lot of Things Don't

How much of what even top performers do is just convention, and makes little difference to the outcome? The true story above, which my Dad witnessed to his great amusement, shows what most keen amateur sportspeople and musicians figure out eventually. The real success factors can't be bough in from the outside; you have to develop them from within (see Figure 8.1).

One client I discussed this issue with, a keen golfer, summed up the issue facing the naïve equipment enthusiast like this: 'All the gear, but no idea.' The right gear unquestionably helps, but it's not 'it'. Similarly, to return to the football club example from Chapter 1, buying the best striker in the world won't, on its own, help much with the teamwork required to orchestrate a win.

Principle Six: Find the Few Things That Really Make a Difference

Conventional view		Reality	
Doesn't make a difference	Makes a difference	Doesn't make a difference	Makes a difference
Wisdom	Your own bat Correct uniform	Braces, Street shoes, The 'in crowd's' approval	Level of skill, Experience

Figure 8.1 Differences that make a difference: table tennis

The worst kind of waste

You don't have to look far to see business parallels. Consider for example:

- **Bloated software packages.** These come loaded with features that most people never learn of, let alone use, and impose the added waste of running slowly, sapping memory, and because of their complexity, being prone to lock up or crash.

- **Markets full of undifferentiated products.** It's tempting to follow the crowd when defining 'what good looks like'. But how many of the standard trappings really affect results, and how many are just the way everyone does it? How much time do people spend copying what other people claim is 'best practice' with effects that are marginal at best? One car manufacturer lined up a bunch of family cars into a hangar. All the cars were silver. One was its own model; the others were built by competitors. Oh, and they took the identifying badges off. Without those badges, the manufacturer's people couldn't tell their own model from the others.

- **Over-engineered hardware.** Some products may be really cool to the engineers that built them, but be unusable at anywhere near their potential. The automotive industry again provides clear examples. I like a track day as much as anyone, but consider the waste represented by cars with capabilities that would be illegal, dangerous and beyond the skills of most customers to exploit on the road. And recall the truck example from Chapter 7: engineers

	Conventional view		Reality
Doesn't make a difference	Makes a difference	Doesn't make a difference	Makes a difference
Seats	Subtle upgrades in already phenomenal power delivery profiles	Marginal gains in fuel efficiency	Ergonomic seating

Figure 8.2 Differences that make a difference: trucks

were obsessed by small gains in engine efficiency but the haulage company wanted comfortable seats so that expensive drivers wouldn't be paid to sit at home with backache (see Figure 8.2).

Lower performance may be more valuable

GE had been trying for years to sell premium-priced ultrasound scanners in China. The problem was that 90% of hospitals couldn't afford them, and after trying for ten years, GE's ultrasound sales were a disappointing $5 million.

In response, the company designed a scanner just for the Chinese market. By focusing on essentials, the local team came up with a hand-held version for $15,000, around 10% of the premium price. Its performance wasn't as good as the premium scanner, but it was affordable, easy to carry and easy to use – ideal for rural areas. Between 2002 and 2008, GE's ultrasound sales in China grew from $5 million to nearly $300 million.

And here's an interesting twist: it turned out that people in developed markets liked the stripped-down scanners, too. GE now sells them in the US and other developed countries for use in ambulances and operating rooms – previously untapped markets for which the premium scanners were over-engineered, and so impractical.[1] (As I often say in my talks: users, not technologists or managers, determine the value of products.)

Questions to consider:

- Where are we incurring costs to deliver things – features, services, extras – that the customer isn't noticing, or simply doesn't care about?
- How well do we understand the job the customer is trying to do through using our product or service, and how well do we understand their criteria?
- Are our technical people indulging themselves rather than meeting user requirements?
- How might we advantageously differentiate ourselves by *removing* features from our offerings? Could we even earn a premium on the 'less is more' principle?

The customer may crave less than you think

In one customer service call centre, customer satisfaction was worryingly low. The call centre manager had tried various things to fix the problem. He tried training programmes, incentive schemes and clever scripts. These, he hoped, would promulgate 'best practices' and 'drive' behaviour. These had been ineffective, as efforts to 'drive' behaviour often are.

One of my colleagues moved the focus of attention away from the operator and paid it to the customer point of view. What, he enquired, did customers hate about the call centre? The answers offered no startling insights. Customers said they hated:

1 'the scripted sing-song voices when the operators answer the phone,' and
2 the fact that 'when operators don't immediately know the answer, they say they'll get back to me, and then don't.'

The answer was simply to reverse those two things. This was done by:

1 providing basic voice training of the sort given to actors; they taught the operators to use a warm, downward inflection, rather than an annoying sing-song;

2 making sure operators made firm appointments for call-backs and fulfilled them.

That was it. Satisfaction was comprehensively turned around by paying attention to the two things customers were paying attention to. All the earlier work on incentives and clever scripts was at best irrelevant.

When Less Is More

'Less is more' is a cliché for a reason: it's often the right direction to go. Less isn't *always* more however. Figure 8.3 helps to sort things out.

The GE scanner story is an example of Frugal Innovation, itself the title of an inspiring book by Navi Radjou and Jaideep Prabhu. Radjou and Prabhu tell fascinating stories about innovative thinkers in emerging markets, creating high-quality products with limited resources. The authors show how practices which they term *jugaad* – a

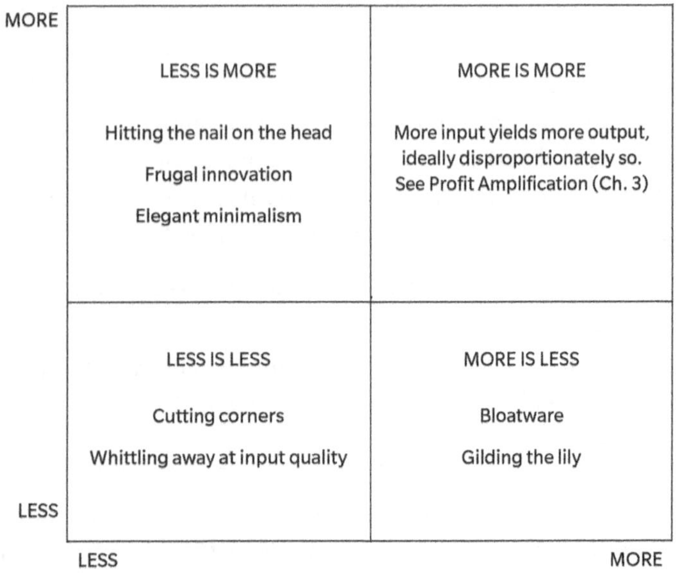

	LESS IS MORE Hitting the nail on the head Frugal innovation Elegant minimalism	MORE IS MORE More input yields more output, ideally disproportionately so. See Profit Amplification (Ch. 3)
	LESS IS LESS Cutting corners Whittling away at input quality	MORE IS LESS Bloatware Gilding the lily

(Y-axis: LESS → MORE; X-axis: LESS → MORE)

Figure 8.3 When less is more

Principle Six: Find the Few Things That Really Make a Difference

Hindi word meaning 'an improvised solution born from ingenuity and cleverness' – create growth and can offer opportunities to reduce waste, increase sustainability and boost profit, not only in emerging markets but in mature ones as well.

The day after I started reading the book, I ran a seminar for charity CEOs about how to start with what works. I gave the participants an exercise based on the Car Wash framework we met in Chapter 3: they had to generate a series of Options 1, 2, 3 etc., which would deliver increasing value to their beneficiaries and funders, while amplifying the charities' surpluses and so their reinvestment.

While the CEOs were working, I recalled the book I'd been reading. After they had finished I said, 'Okay, charities are always resource constrained, so now let's try some 'frugal innovation'. Let's come up with an Option Zero.' Start with an actual car wash.

'How do we do that?'

'Well, Option 2 adds elements to Option 1. So Option Zero must subtract elements.'

'But the only elements in Option 1 are soap and water'

I replied, 'let's subtract the water then.'

This was greeted with general scepticism. I attempted a recovery:

'Okay, maybe it doesn't work for the car wash, but try it for your charities and see what happens'.

Somewhat grudgingly the leaders turned to their task.

Meanwhile, I got curious, so I Googled 'waterless car wash.' To my delight I found an Indian product, called Eco-Touch, available on Amazon. Each spray can of Eco-Touch is good for ten car washes, and because the formulation is both biodegradable and waterless, it is actually more ecologically friendly for a country where water is a much scarcer resource than rainy England.

Of course I was a bit smug when I announced my discovery to the group. But the technique of Option Zero has remained in my repertoire as a sometimes very useful addition to the Car Wash technique – see Figure 8.4.

Start with what works

Bundle \ Element	Soap	Rinse	Water blaster	Underbody	Dry	Wax	Value	Price
Three	*	*	*	*	*	*	Spotless and shiny	£8
Two	*	*	*	*			Thorough clean	£6
One	*	*					Basic clean	£4
Zero	*						Basic clean without wasting water	£10 for 10 washes

Figure 8.4 Option Zero

Exercise
Option Zero

Here are the steps:

- Using the Car Wash framework, cast one of your existing offerings as an Option 1 (see Chapter 4 for a reminder).
- By all means explore Options 2, 3 (and even 4, 5 and 6) to broaden out your thinking about what you can provide, and what your customers would get value from.
- Now experiment with removing apparently crucial elements from various options – what ideas does this suggest?
- How could you test these ideas in the outside world?

Seven More Ways to Find the Few Things That Make a Difference

Once you get into the right mindset, there are many ways to home in on the factors that make the real difference. Here are seven to consider.

1. Demand answers to the question, 'So what?'

It's a terrible waste to add features that the customer doesn't notice. Customers can only prefer something if they can distinguish it from alternatives. We've already met examples of this in the book:

- The family car manufacturer we discussed earlier, who lined up a bunch of their competitors – all in silver – and took the badges off. It turned out the manufacturer's own staff couldn't identify their own car. Think of the waste that must have gone into its design.
- The fuel haulier, who was left cold by technical differences in truck design. While these were exciting to an engineer, what the haulier cared about was seat ergonomics and high availability. MAN Trucks realised this and secured an advantage.
- *The Times* newspaper (in Chapter 3), who offered so many options that potential subscribers perceived it all as noise and just gave up. Ogilvy redesigned the offer into three clear choices and subscriptions jumped.

Some engineers will absolutely hate the message I'm giving you here. Features they have obsessed over may be utterly irrelevant to a buying decision or ongoing satisfaction. Again, think of all the complex computer code in unused features of popular word processors. Someone 'invested' huge hours, and presumably an expensive education and high salary, into an act of futility.

What to do?

- Ask, 'So what? So what? So what?' to the point of discomfort and beyond. I use the 'So what?' question to torture engineers who want to add unneeded features. I usually try to soften it by saying, 'So, just so I'm clear, what is the need that this feature fulfils for the user?' It's amazing how hard they find it to come up with an answer. (See Chapter 2 – getting stuck in existing categories).
- Test hypotheses about the value of differences. Apply the methods in Chapter 6 ('Let the world teach you') to test hypotheses such as 'The customer will be able to tell the difference' and 'The customer will care about the difference'.

Ultimately, the only differences worth anything are those that make a difference to the user.

2. Resist the temptation to over-complicate

As a child I remember being allowed to stay up past 9 p.m. to watch the Apollo moon landings. As an adult, understanding more about what those missions took, and having seen the Lunar Module at the Smithsonian in Washington, DC, I actually find Apollo more mind-boggling now than I did then!

The US won that particular space race but, taken as a whole, the Russian programme is equally impressive and, because it was not as well funded, offers thought-provoking perspectives about innovation with limited resources. There's a great story that during the 1960s, NASA spent millions of dollars to develop a pen that could write in zero gravity, while the Russians simply handed their cosmonauts pencils. This is a story that deserves to be true, but unfortunately, a *Scientific American* article confirms that it's a myth. It still makes a good point, however, and does capture something of the Russian approach: a BBC 'From our own correspondent' report showed that the Russian space programme has often had to rely on ingenuity rather than funds. Today's Russian space technology is a robust mixture of both sophisticated and pragmatically low-tech. For example, the BBC correspondent reported:

> 'In order to dock to the space station the [Soyuz] commander uses an optical periscope which sticks out of the side.
>
> 'Why not a camera,' I ask?
>
> 'Why make it complicated?' replies the colonel.'

This focus on results rather than the seductions of technology for its own sake is surely a key to the robustness of Soyuz. It's an old design after all – the first version launched in 1966 – yet it can launch in a blizzard. By contrast, the Space Shuttle – undoubtedly a magnificent achievement, and probably the most complex machine ever built by humans – would be delayed by relatively light winds.

There are no national monopolies on either technological sophistication or ingenious pragmatism. However, there does seem to be a widespread temptation to want to use the cleverest technology even when there is a simpler, cheaper, lower-risk, more robust way to get the same result.

What about the design of business processes and products? How many bloated product portfolios offer incomprehensible variants – across a range of tightly packed price points – distinguished only by unnecessary extra features? It's worth considering how much technological and methodological overkill there is in any business.

3. Win the 'No Talent' battle

My colleague Craig Preston is a high-performance coach. A former graduate and later, member of staff at the Royal Military Academy, Sandhurst, he has held executive positions in logistics, financial services and elite sport, including being the first Head of People Development at the Rugby Football Union. He also played senior level rugby in the All Ireland League.

Craig and I were discussing my conversation with Paul Faulkner, former-CEO of Aston Villa Football Club (Chapter 1). You'll remember that Paul had identified with start with what works, saying it was just like running a football club.

Craig made the connect to rugby, where the Exeter Chiefs have become a dominant force, not because of individual superstars, but because of what the coach Rob Hunter describes as an emphasis on ensuring the team is the best at all the factors of rugby which require no talent – things like get up from the floor and get into position quicker than other teams, being fitter than the other teams and having better nutrition. In Hunter's words: 'We win the no talent battle'.

Craig then reflected on his own experiences in what was then the All Ireland League.

It was, strangely, the easiest rugby I ever played. Because I could predict and depend on what my teammates would do, I could plan my own play. I knew that if the ball went to the fly half he would kick or pass it, reliably and quickly, so I could act on that basis, safe in the knowledge of what would happen.

At a lower level of rugby, I'd be wondering, 'Will he take the kick? Will he wait a couple of seconds to set up, or to make the correct decision? Will he botch the kick? That all creates doubt in the team, slowing down your own movement and decision-making, and putting them on the back foot. And of course, it was the same in the military.

It's the same in business, too. If everyone agrees to have done a bunch of jobs by Friday so that a pitch can go out on Monday, can you depend on it happening? It makes a huge difference. Factors such as being on time, finishing on time, reading the papers before the meeting, fulfilling commitments. . . these rely on little or no talent. Literally anyone can improve them. Yet without them, talent can't express itself.

4. Learn from Colonel Boyd and the F-16

I am a great admirer of the work of Col. John R. Boyd (he was an ace fighter pilot, dog-fighting instructor, engineer, military strategist, historian of science, and often unacknowledged influence in the military and business worlds. I highly recommend Robert Coram's biography: *Boyd*).[2]

Boyd was called in to consult on a jet fighter engine project (the aircraft in question became the F-16) and the engineering team was getting heavily bogged down trying to amalgamate their three favourite engines into one design. They were bringing with them their assumptions based on previous projects, and as a consequence couldn't reconcile their ideas in a way that would work. The engine they were headed towards building would be

Principle Six: Find the Few Things That Really Make a Difference

too heavy and too low-powered to get off the ground, let alone meet the desired performance for a manoeuvrable dog-fighter. Everything was too complicated, and the debate about trade-offs was going in circles.

Picking his moment, Boyd, a forceful and charismatic presence, said essentially: 'Let's assume that a jet engine is just a pipe. Cold air goes in the front, hot air comes out of the back – we call that thrust. As to what happens in between – all bets are off.'

Released from their assumptions and wrangling, the team proceeded to produce an engine that exceeded the required performance criteria (see Figure 8.5).

You can use the same pattern to redesign a product, service, or business model:

1. Refocus on the need you are trying to meet – what are the absolute minimum requirements for something to qualify as a solution? What has to come out? And what has to go in? Make this list as short as possible.

2. What else needs to be true in addition: things like absolute level of output? Input–output ratio? Suitable ROI measure? Again keep this list to a minimum.

3. What are actually 'want to haves' and 'like to haves' masquerading as 'must haves'? Make a list. This list will be longer than the true musts – keep going until everyone has dried up.

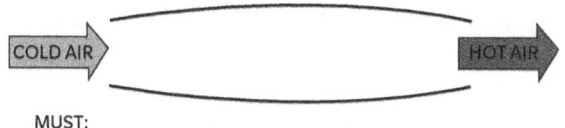

MUST:
Take cold air in the front and send hot air out of the back

WANT:
Thrust of 23,000 - 30,000 lbf
Fuel consumption better than 90 (lb/h)/lbf
Thrust-to-weight ratio of 7.8:1

Figure 8.5 Boyd's approach to designing a jet engine

4 Set aside everything except the essential function and musts (i.e. your answers to 1 and 2) – get a blank sheet of paper and start designing from there.
5 Protect your new design from any of the considerations from the third list for as long as possible.

5. Focus everyone on ROI

Politicians of all stripes will try to convince you of their worth by telling you how much money they have poured into a particular strategic area, usually health, education or policing. It is much rarer to hear them talking about the increase in value they got back for the extra money (never mind that the money they so generously have 'given' was not theirs in the first place – this is a basic confusion for most politicians and they are not likely to make the effort to achieve clarity!).

Politicians do seem to dislike the inconvenience of considering the whole picture, preferring to select the most flattering bit of the story. It's much easier to claim credit for effort – especially that of other people – rather than results.

Businesspeople may find it easy to scoff: after all, business is all about results, right?

Well, businesspeople also confuse inputs and outputs.

Box 8.1
Focusing everyone on ROI. Some questions to consider:

How did the actual marketing cost you last reported come about?

- Was it the amount you needed to spend to achieve the strategic result you sought?
- Did you look for the ideas that would give you the most bang for your buck and then allocate the bucks?

> Or was the spend allocated in the year previously, therefore acting as a powerful constraint on your marketing possibilities, so that for example:
>
> - if you developed mid-year a potential project with an unexpectedly high ROI – a desired output – you had no way of increasing your investment to take advantage in time?
> - because people had a fixed budget, they were psyched out of innovating more effective projects in the first place?
> - your overall marketing emphasis enshrined a strategy at least a year and a half out of date?
>
> And what about other areas:
>
> - Do you give your learning and development people a fixed budget that they then use up with whichever courses, programmes and modish trainers they can find? Or do you start with the behaviour and skills required by your business model and then figure out how most effectively to create them?
> - Does a similar 'logic' apply to other areas such as IT and R&D?

People always find ways to spend their pre-allocated budgets. In contrast, I know businesses that have achieved dramatic results by drilling everyone to ask and answer the following simple question in response to any request for money: 'What is the return on this investment?'

And I'm not just talking about large-scale project appraisal; I'm talking about every request for funds: perks, expense reimbursements, travel to in-person meetings, gadgets, bits of software, paperclips, and so on.

The point is not to stop people spending. Far from it – the point is to encourage ROI thinking, which is possible at all levels. The more you encourage it, the more it becomes a habit, and then affects the overall quality of debate and decision-making.

Give it a try: at first people might be taken aback, and find it hard to answer when you ask 'What's the return on this?', but if you persevere, and coach them a bit, they will start to anticipate you and start bringing you ideas you'll be delighted to say 'Yes' to.

6. Keeping the focus on outputs...

People often think their job is done when they've completed their inputs, but success all has to do with outputs.

If you go and see a comedian, you don't care how much work they put into writing their act and practising it. You care that you laugh. If you don't laugh, it doesn't matter that the comedian sweated and put a lot of time and money into the creation of the act.

For whatever reason though – maybe educators give too much credit to students for showing their work even if the answer is wrong, maybe being able to say 'But I worked hard' is often an acceptable excuse, maybe there's a vestigial Puritanism that values hard work for its own sake – the fact is that there is a focus on inputs.

In a business setting, the kind of inputs I'm thinking of might be:

- making 20 sales calls a day (the output would be actual profitable sales);
- implementing a new performance management IT system (the output would be higher performing, more promotable people);
- writing reports and PowerPoint presentations (the output could be making a good decision and getting support for the follow-through implementation).

This isn't just about individual productivity, it's also about teams and organisations as a whole: most meeting agendas I see are lists of issues. And issues are ... inputs.

So if you lead a team or organisation, the challenge is to keep everyone's focus on the outputs. Here are three of the fastest ways:

- If you must hold a meeting, then instead of an agenda that's a long list of issues, have an agenda that's a very short list of objectives, with clear evidence criteria for when you have succeeded. For example:

- Objective: To decide which of three new product ideas to pursue.
- Evidence: We will have a named individual who will be responsible for managing the project, with an allocated initial budget, and a date and time for them to provide an initial report on progress.
- Delegate responsibility for producing results, not merely for following a sequence of steps in a process.
- Make sure that people who produce results are conspicuously recognised and rewarded above and beyond those who just completed the checklist. The rewards don't always have to be financial. The people you are looking for will be most encouraged by juicier assignments, high-level mentoring or promotions.

7. Sort out real vs espoused priorities

I once attended a board meeting of a struggling media company as an observer. The Chairman was a tough-as-nails turnaround specialist. I vividly remember him swivelling away from the PowerPoint presentation to round on the directors.

'We've been talking about this new product for eighteen months,' he admonished. 'So where is it?'

The directors squirmed, and responded with an ineffectual: 'It's still a priority, but. . .'

The Chairman held his head in his hands, as if to stop the steam from coming out of his ears.

The phrase 'It's still a priority, but. . .' is what is technically known as 'Bulls**t.' There's a big difference between real priorities and espoused priorities. If you want to know what the espoused priorities are, look at what people say in their PowerPoint decks and Annual Reports. But if you want to know if it's a real priority, *pay attention to what actually happens.*

Don't wait until it's too late. Ask yourself the following:

> 'If X were, really, seriously an active priority of this business, what three to five things would absolutely be happening NOW that would prove it?'

For example, if selling the new product really is a priority, don't wait until you can see the sales numbers. That's far too late. Also, don't take the sales manager's word for it.

Ask: 'What must be happening *today* if that new product is a priority?' This could be that:

- Email correspondence shows follow-up on meetings with buyers where the product was discussed.
- Technical experts on the new products have been asked to accompany sales people on calls.
- Samples are being requested from the new products team.

. . . or a host of other bits of evidence depending on your unique situation.

Results don't appear out of a vacuum. Any goal presupposes certain actions that must happen first. To make sure your organisation is serious about its stated priorities, look for these actions – they offer much better information than any PowerPoint progress report.

In Conclusion: Don't Let Means Triumph Over Ends

If Friedrich Nietzsche hadn't been a great philosopher, he would have made a pretty good consultant (I leave you to decide whether this was a missed opportunity. . .).

Here's an example of his perspicacity:

> 'During the journey we commonly forget its goal. Almost every profession is chosen and commenced as a means to an end but continued as an end in itself. Forgetting our objectives is the most frequent of all acts of stupidity.'

Not one to mince words was Professor Nietzsche, as I am sure you will agree. But how does this apply to our business considerations?

You will probably spend a fair proportion of your time this week sitting in meetings. How much of what is discussed will be about activities that have become untethered from the goals they were once intended to achieve?

Vulnerable areas include research, budgeting & planning exercises, organisational development activities, over-elaborate system implementations, processes and procedures, not to mention the meetings themselves.

For example, look out for things like this:

- **People regard divisional 'strategic planning' as a form-filling exercise to keep 'corporate' happy,** rather than a way that they identify and act on the most promising growth opportunities.

- **'Targets' are achieved – and bonuses consequently paid – while goals remain unmet.** This often results from clumsy use of balanced scorecards and dashboards: you find elaborate chains of metrics detached from the real objective (e.g. 'short call centre queue length' is rewarded, which leads to operators hurrying customers off the line, causing a *decrease* in satisfaction. *But* the target is met).

- **Data gathering is repeated every week/month/year without resulting in new actions.** A common example: surveys are started as a way of ensuring morale, then, when the results show that people are unhappy, the feedback is suppressed or watered down (making everyone less happy still). That's bad enough, but then the survey runs the same time the next year!

- **There's lots of 'preparing to get ready to change'.** For example, getting staff certified in some methodology or other is called a 'deliverable', or happy sheet scores are taken as evidence of achievement. *Passing a milestone is not the same as reaching the destination.* Being underprepared is silly, of course, but overdoing preparation just delays any result-producing action and it's one of the most tempting and time-consuming traps in change management.

The remedy – which I grant sounds incredibly obvious – lies in two questions: 'Why?' and – once again – 'So What?' as in,

'Why are we (still) doing this?'
And,
'Given this research/set of filled-in forms/survey/data . . . *So what?*'

It sounds obvious, but evidence all around us shows that this kind of focus is nonetheless elusive. Leaders have to keep their organisations focused on results, not on procedures which have become over-elaborate, or which may have been a good idea once but are now past their sell-by date.

One of Nietzsche's books had the evocative title: *'Human, All Too Human'* and certainly that's a fair assessment of the tendency to forget the goal and become engrossed in the intricacies of a task. A leader has to stay aware of this all-too-human tendency and be vigilant: is the busy-ness actually making a real difference?

Chapter 9

Principle Seven: Use *Very* Plain Words to Describe What You Want

Throughout the book, we've talked about bringing new and more focused value to customers by starting with what works. As the value you offer changes, your organisation will have to keep up. When people are talking about a change that's needed in their organisation, they bandy about words like *transformation, communication* and *engagement* and everyone nods. But what the heck do these words mean? Unless you get really clear, you'll be tempted to buy in generic 'transformation programmes', 'communication trainings' and 'engagement tools'. These generic 'solutions' are often time-consuming and disruptive. They are at best blunt instruments and at worst irrelevant to the real issues affecting your business. In contrast, when you describe those issues and your desired outcomes in very plain words, you may be surprised to find that your own people can sort them out with minimal outside assistance.

Vague Language and 'Artificial' Intelligence

An old university joke defines *a lecture* as 'a device for transferring information from the notes of the lecturer to the notes of the student, without it passing through the minds of either'. Just because a bunch of people are doing something which sounds and looks intelligent is no guarantee that it is! Management has evolved a plethora of intelligent-sounding abstractions (also known as corporate-speak, or management BS) that often does little more than create illusory consensus. If you are responsible for results, then this kind of 'artificial' intelligence won't do. It will just create value-sapping confusion, error and frustration. In this chapter I will flag up some of the ways this shows up, and equip you to detect and correct it, and so to engage more of the real – possibly untapped – intelligence in your organisation. (In this regard, I find there are broadly two types of management consultants: those who add to the pile of BS and those who spend their time patiently helping their clients dismantle it so they can see their way clearly to the results they seek.)

Bewitched by language

Free-floating abstractions abound at work, creating the appearance of intelligent discussion where there may be very little. The vernacular term for this, of course, is 'bulls**t'. Here's a typical example: as a consultant on a project in an investment bank, I was asked to meet a senior IT project manager by the COO. Let's call the COO Jane. Jane was very keen for this meeting to happen, although she was vague about the reason. The manager – 'Mike' – was quick to make sure I knew his credentials, previous blue-chip employers, ratings and 'black belts'. He then started to talk an incomprehensible (to me anyway) stream of apparently meaningful words and phrases – I remember one was something like 'compliant project governance architecture'. Even with a background in software engineering, I was left without a clue what he was saying, although it all sounded strangely impressive.

Next time I saw the COO, she wasted little time on getting to the question that was bugging her. She phrased her enquiry as innocently as possible:

> 'So, how did you get on with Mike?'

This was one of those little moments of truth for any consultant. I took a deep breath:

> 'To be honest Jane, I didn't understand a bloody word he said.'
>
> 'Thank you!' she replied, with a look of vindication.

I went on:

> 'Actually I suspect he's full of BS.'
>
> 'That's what I think too,' said Jane, but he seems to have a lot of people impressed. He has some influential supporters round here, but I think he is wasting our time and resources.'

As we discussed Mike further we tried to account for the positive perceptions of him. Maybe some people were just worried in case they looked stupid for not understanding him – and maybe others just let the abstractions slide by because they were busy, and he sounded confident and meaningful. And yes, we even considered that maybe we were simply wrong about him. (Subsequent events proved that we were not, however, and he left under a cloud.)

Mike was an extreme example, but he had got a long way at some big-name businesses because, if someone has the knack, talking in terms of free-floating abstractions (empowerment initiative, leadership benchmarking, governance architecture, conceptual vision, business model evolution, world-class operational excellence) sounds meaningful *whether the listener can figure out what the speaker is referring to or not.*

In fact it is quite possible for people to 'converse', back and forth, apparently meaningfully, almost purely in terms of undefined, usually multisyllabic abstract nouns and adjectives. An observer or newcomer will have the feeling of being left out of an important and significant discussion. I've seen this in most organisations, in every industry I've worked in. The result is often a comedy of errors, or more usually, just errors.

Just because it *seems* clever...

ELIZA was the name of Joseph Weisenbaum's classic early artificial intelligence computer program, which parodied a 'non-directive' psychotherapist. ELIZA worked by simply selecting some portion of what you had just typed in and using the selected portion to build its next question. So if you typed:

'I am depressed'

Eliza might reply:

'Oh, I am sorry to hear that you are depressed. When did it start?'

It is easy enough to see how ELIZA works: basically through a set of rules telling it to shuffle words about (to convert 'I' to 'you', 'am' to 'are' and so on). A few tens of such rules got the system a long way.

Replicating ELIZA is an undergraduate-level assignment and versions exist on the Internet. If you try one you will find that it's amazing how convincing such 'word shuffling' can be. In fact, because people like to anthropomorphise, many who interacted with it judged the original ELIZA program genuinely intelligent – Weisenbaum's secretary liked to discuss her problems with ELIZA because she felt it listened better than most humans. The credulity with which people projected real intelligence onto ELIZA disturbed Weizenbaum and led him to write a book on the limits of computers.

Now consider the following dialogue (which I have only heard about a gazillion times in conversations among managers about organisational issues):

> 'We have a sales problem.'
> "Ok, let's get some sales training in.'
>
> 'We have a problem with staff empowerment.'
> 'This empowerment programme is specially designed to do that.'
>
> 'We have a credit control problem.'
> 'Let's buy this new credit control software.'

In each case, the 'ELIZA pattern' is simply to take the word 'problem' out of the description of the issue and substitute in a word such as 'training', 'programme', or 'software'. Bingo, you've got your answer.

This is what I called a Saviour Solution in Chapter 2. If you assert an 'ELIZA prescription' confidently, it's amazing how often people will nod uncritically and move on to the next item on the agenda, feeling sure they have dealt with the issue. It looks like a decision has been taken. The trouble is that it's been taken without the issue passing through the minds of the parties discussing it.

Consider the first example above – a requirement to improve sales. Sales *training* may sound like a good idea, but it will be totally ineffective in these common situations:

- timid salespeople unsuited to the role;
- outdated products which customers are ignoring in favour of the competition;
- an unfair formal incentive system;

- discouraging informal incentives;
- a sales manager who is playing favourites;
- hard-to-use tools and processes;
- influential role models who are conspicuously thriving even though they violate company values;
- outdated beliefs about the 'way we do things here';
- a divisive manager you should have sorted out ages ago.

Will an ELIZA prescription – a generic solution such as a bought-in course, programme or system – meet your unique requirement? It's hit-and-miss at best.

It's extremely tempting to think you can get a template solution off the shelf. The problem is that the tendency to pigeonhole problems and solutions can lead you in the wrong direction. Almost all management situations have familiar and predictable elements in them, true enough, but they also have unique elements, and it is *those* that are usually the most significant ones from the perspective of getting a result.

Mike-the-project-governance-architect and ELIZA may seem intelligent, but it's an illusion. The illusion is based on the all-too-human tendency to uncritically impute intelligence where there is nothing but a set of superficial but unreliable cues.

It's important to realise that we can all fall foul of this kind of uncritical acceptance – in fact, talk to professional close-up magicians and they will tell you that the easiest people to fool are the sophisticated audiences (the heroes of prestidigitation are those who can do kids' parties – a much tougher crowd altogether).

Plain Word Techniques

Here are some disciplines to help you to sidestep the bewitching effects of 'artificial' intelligence and ELIZA-prescribed generic solutions, and so improve the quality of your organisation's evolution.

1. Be wary of pre-packaged solutions looking for problems

These include generic training programmes, management fads and personality tests. Ask salespeople, internal recommenders and 'experts': 'How do you know it will work *in our specific situation*?'

2. Release your inner pedant

Even at the risk of being thought ignorant or pedantic, be prepared to ask two simple questions when 'specialists' use jargon, or indeed when a free-floating abstraction drifts into any discussion: 'What do you mean, exactly?' and 'Can you give me an example?'

3. Neutralise attempted one-upmanship

If you are dealing with the kind of bluff operator who seems to be implying that if you don't follow the jargon you must be less intelligent, try the following: 'I've heard that terminology used in a slightly different context, but it doesn't seem to have the same meaning that you are giving it – just explain, what's the difference as you are using it between a compliant and non-compliant governance architecture?'

4. Use the troubleshooter documentary technique

Too many changes are described in vague language. We want to 'go from good to great', or 'get to the next level', or we want to resolve 'communication issues' or 'get people to take ownership'. These are all fine as starting points, but they need to be nailed down if you want more than vague results.

I will often respond to statements such as those above by saying the following: 'Imagine we did a Before-and-After documentary about the change process. The film crew would film the current situation, and then would come back once the change has occurred and film again. What differences would you want to see and hear on the two playbacks, so that you said to me: 'LOOK! LISTEN! That's the difference. That's how I know they have taken ownership (or that we're now 'great' or at 'the next level', or whatever the objective might be)?' Figure 9.1 provides a template for organising the answers.

Troubleshooter Documentary technique

Instructions: Imagine we made a fly-on-the-wall documentary which filmed the business before and after a successful alignment to a new strategy. What would we see and hear on the tape? What would change between the first and last episodes? Think about customer/client experience, meetings and decision making, delegation, sales meeting ... ? What would be the impact on financial performance, reputation, ability to attract and retain good people. . . ?

Before	After	Impact on the business

Bass Clusker Consulting

@Andrew Bass 2008. All Rights Reserved.

Figure 9.1 The Troubleshooter Documentary technique

Why is there also a column for Business Impact? Because the impact is what will determine how much effort, resource and urgency should be put into the change. Too often, people spend a lot of time and energy on improvements of only marginal consequence, but don't make big enough investments in things that would make a huge difference.

5. 'De-Nominalise' the management jargon

You can use the TV Documentary technique to make all sorts of management jargon concrete and understandable. Essentially, you're taking abstract management nouns and turn them back into verbs[1] by asking: 'How do we do that?' For example:

- *Leadership*: Who is leading whom to do what? How are they doing it? What happens as a result?
- *Engagement*: Who is engaging with whom? How specifically are they doing it?
- *Transformation*: What specifically is being transformed into what? How specifically? How will we know it's been transformed?
- *Agility*: What is being done in an agile way? By whom? How specifically?

In all cases, whether or not you use a TV Documentary framework, you're looking for a clear and unambiguous answer to the question: 'What do we need to see and hear to know it's happening the way we need it to?'

Use Plain Words to Tell *Others* What You Want

Once you've clarified what you want, you will usually have to get that over to other people. There's a lot of potential for miscommunication here, so finding the right words is vital.

Let's look first at what doesn't work. For example, here is a genuine Fortune 500 mission statement (I'll maintain the company's anonymity):

> 'We are a market-focused, process-centered organisation that develops and delivers innovative solutions to our customers, consistently outperforms our peers, produces predictable earnings for our shareholders, and provides a dynamic and challenging environment for our employees.'

This is a long way from the plain words we worked on finding earlier in the chapter. It's so abstract and anodyne – and similar to a thousand other such statements – that it lacks any focus. It does nothing to help decision-making at any level in the organisation.

In contrast, Google declare in their mission statement their intention to gather the world's information and make it useful and accessible to all.

The beauty of plain words like this is that they can be used by people to make intelligent and strategically aligned choices. Google employs creative and brilliant people with wide and varied interests, and it encourages them to innovate. It would be easy for them to go off on what the lawyers call 'frolics of their own'. But instead, they can say 'I have this idea, but is it helping organise the world's information?' and act accordingly. That means Google Books is in, as is Google Calendar. But what about the company's more recent efforts in pursuit of glucose-sensing contact lenses or longevity? It's significant that the company reorganised as Alphabet, with Google as a division. This allows the wider business to pursue a range of other bets without diluting the core that drove its growth and still supplies the lion's share of returns.

How an articulated essence shapes results

Figure 9.2 shows a chain from the leader's strategic intent to the results produced. Working from the bottom, it says that results follow from behaviours, which follow from decisions, which are shaped by the articulation of the purpose and priorities – the intent – of the

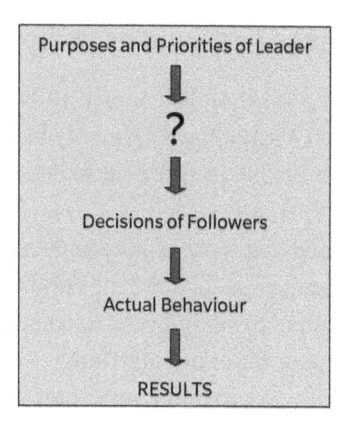

```
Purposes and Priorities of Leader
          ↓
          ?
          ↓
    Decisions of Followers
          ↓
      Actual Behaviour
          ↓
        RESULTS
```

Figure 9.2 How clearly are you articulating your intent?

leader. If you try to articulate that intent in vague terms, you can only hope for vague results.

An articulated distilled essence creates brand-aligned customer experiences

Google's mission statement conveys the essence of its overall intent in plain words that guide decisions throughout the organisation to make decisions. IKEA provides another excellent example of an essence that shapes both product strategy and brand behaviours. In their case, the essence is captured in their stated vision to improve everyday life for the many.

While this clearly relates to decisions about their product range, I found that it extends to their after-sales service too. When I bought some bookcases from IKEA and got them home, I found that one of the backboards had split. I couldn't be sure, but based on the shape of the hole, it looked like I broke it when transporting it home. I went back to the store prepared for an explanation, and if necessary to put my hand in my pocket to buy a replacement. But the assistant took one look and said: 'I'll get you another.' No discussion of what might have happened to the board. It certainly made my 'everyday life' easier.

A well-articulated essence is not an idea that's just for huge companies either, as we'll see next.

An articulated essence guides daily behaviour

The Vision Express organisation has nearly 400 retail optician stores in the UK operating on a franchise model. My local store is operated by an energetic French entrepreneur called Benoit. It's very successful.

Ben is very conscious that most of his employees are younger than his core customer base (i.e. people like me coming in for our varifocals!). He says, 'I tell all of my employees to treat those customers the way you would treat your Mum or your Dad.'

That means 'take the care to make sure their glasses are *right*: they look right, they don't pinch, they're polished correctly.' It means: 'don't try to sell them something they don't need, but *do* recommend something that, although it may be more expensive, will be better for them. And just be patient while they are trying to make decisions about frames and lenses and so on.'

'Treat them like your Mum or your Dad.' It doesn't sound like much, but it is an effective guide to behaviour that – without attempting to dictate every detail – captures the essence of Benoit's approach in plain words. It shapes the whole experience of shopping in his branch, and ensures wonderful repeat business and referrals. And combined with Benoit's *je ne sais quoi* and his talent at buying fashionable and interesting frames, it's meant that he has on multiple occasions won the *Manager of the Year* award for being the most profitable store in the country.

Articulating your business's essence

The essence of a business is best captured in vivid stories and word pictures. There are at least five types:

- **'War stories' or anecdotes about moments of truth:** FedEx famously has loads of stories about heroic efforts to deliver parcels – these stories provide role models by proxy.
- **Instantiated values:** One professional services firm made energetic efforts to illustrate its new list of values by finding real examples in plain words. In the case of the value *client service*,

it found and spread the story of clients who got lost on the way to a meeting and were rescued personally by an associate who drove out to them and led them back to the firm's office. The client has never stopped talking about it, tells anyone who will listen, and wouldn't dream of taking their advisory work anywhere else.

- **Vivid metaphors:** One Japanese car manufacturer (Honda, if memory serves) coordinated a design team by having them think of all design elements as fitting for 'a rugby player in a dinner jacket.'
- **Rallying cries:** Honda again. This time in their 1970s motorcycle war with Yamaha where they galvanised staff with the shout: '*Yamaha wo tsubusu!*' – essentially 'Slaughter Yamaha!' – not necessarily everyone's cup of tea, but effective!
- **Customer testimonials for internal consumption:** In many businesses, employees rarely meet customers. My experience is that they love hearing about them. Customer videos can communicate to your people more vividly than any PowerPoint presentation.

The essence of your business may be masked or hidden by diluting elements. It can, however, be reached through a process of distillation. Once articulated, it can then be focused, giving it disproportionate impact. The bottom line is that people in all roles can only decide and act appropriately if they are clear on how your strategic objectives are meant to play out in the real world – leaders need to articulate the essence of the business in plain words.

Concluding Remarks

When compared to management abstractions, very plain words have many benefits. They will:

- streamline debate about where to use resources;
- reduce ambiguity in uncertain situations;

- direct sales efforts appropriately (Have you ever introduced a hot new product or service only to find that sales people don't sell it? They don't seem to realise why it's important to put effort into it instead of the old stuff);
- guide front-line staff at moments of truth – should they acquiesce to a non-standard customer request, or not? Should they incur a cost to put something right, or not? Should they escalate an issue, or deal with it quickly themselves?

Chapter 10

Principle Eight: Look Beyond 'Us and Them'

Starting with what works relies on making connections among overlooked resources. It asks us to recombine those resources and quickly test the new configurations with customers. That often requires looking past old categories and operating across functional boundaries. And that in turn depends on how we think about relationships between Us and Them.

Us and Them stories abound inside the organisation. Ideally, these stories foster cooperation and synergy. But often they are sources of stress and conflict, making it hard to create joined-up experiences for customers. When sales is blaming production, or managers are blaming engineers, and everybody is blaming IT or finance, it's much tougher to bring fresh ideas to fruition. Let's look at ways to challenge assumptions about Us and Them to create conditions for positive change.

Start with what works

Us and Them

Have you ever been stunned to learn a fact about a coworker that shattered an assumption you had about them? Here are some of the ones I've come across:

- A gentle policy researcher whose hobby was white-collar boxing.
- A school administrator who had long jumped for Great Britain.
- A clinical psychologist who had toured internationally as a backing singer for acts such as Paul Weller and Foreigner.
- An engineer who lived on a smallholding where he bred sheep.
- An introverted computer scientist who played lead guitar in a rock band that regularly played to hordes of tattooed Harley-Davidson-riding bikers.
- A banker who, despite no formal training in the subject, was a regular and active participant in weekly astrophysics seminars at one of the world's top universities.
- A temporary secretary who solved the final clue in a cryptic crossword that had baffled two computer science professors.

No doubt you can make your own list, and it's a great exercise to do so. It can remind you of how restricted our views of others and their talents can be.

Conversely, being on the wrong end of other people's limited view of *us* is bewildering, bemusing and often frustrating. I had a personal experience of this when I was considering what to study at university. I told my headmaster that I was interested in studying automotive engineering. His voice dripped with characteristic contempt: 'I can't imagine you getting your hands dirty, Bass.' He was totally unaware that I had spent my previous two summers working at a local car repair business changing oil filters, adjusting spark plugs and generally getting my hands very dirty indeed. He was oblivious to the fact that, if his car had refused to start, I might have been his best chance to get home before dinner.

When we start to think about *Us and Them*, we put *Them* in a conceptual box. This box says what they are supposed to be able to do, how they are to behave, what the possibilities are. Secretaries are not supposed to be better at tough crosswords than professors, a 'fact' that it gave the temp in my story great delight to subvert. And some professors would have then been angry and might have even 'paid her back' later (though in this case they merely laughed ruefully and probably made sure not to leave their unfinished crosswords anywhere she might find them in future).

We probably can't prevent the tendency to box *Them* in with our assumptions, but we can train ourselves to resist it. If we don't, we risk blinding ourselves to their potential (this is why I'm wary of personality tests in the workplace – they institutionalise the boxing-in process). Putting *Them* in a mental box makes it hard for us to see possibilities for what they could do and how we could relate more productively. What we need are prompts and tools to make us check our assumptions. Here's a simple one.

Exercise
Total Person Inventory

Name	Hobbies, interests, tasks completed in previous jobs etc	So: capabilities	Other implied resources (see chapter five)	What ideas does this suggest?

In consulting assignments, I often meet very able middle- and junior-level people whose contributions essentially make the business work, and do so using skills of which senior managers are blissfully unaware. The *Total Person Inventory* helps direct your attention to the hidden skills you may be missing in others.

Of course, employees are no less prone than their managers to box-in other people. So on the one hand, I've often heard business managers caricature engineers as being inherently uncommercial, discounting the fact that some of the world's most successful businesses were founded by engineers. While on the other hand, engineers criticise senior management for not understanding the technology (I've seen this even when those managers have advanced degrees in the exact technology in question, but don't use their doctoral title for whatever reason).

My point is, of course, that *They* are always so much more than our ideas about them. Our ideas about each other are absolutely central to recognising what works or could work given the chance. Those ideas affect our ability to release potential, and our ability to negotiate changes, both inside the organisation and outside in the marketplace. In this chapter we'll focus on the inside of the organisation. We'll look at customers in the next chapter.

Us and Them get trapped in a deadly embrace

Historically, AW&B was one of three leading producers of aircraft wheels and brakes.[1] In the mid 1950s the company won a contract to supply brakes for a new fighter aircraft. However, the brake did not meet AW&B's promises, and as a result, the company was suspended as a supplier by the OEM (Original Equipment Manufacturer, the organisation responsible for assembling component parts into the final aircraft).

Being suspended was a major hit. It meant not only losses on the original order, but also the even greater loss of continuing business for spare parts.

Principle Eight: Look Beyond 'Us and Them'

A few years later, the same OEM invited bids for the wheels and braking system for a new aircraft. In an attempt to buy itself back in to the business, AW&B put in an especially low-cost bid. The OEM was attracted by the price. They also liked the proposed design, which promised a smaller and lighter brake than was usual.

AW&B got the order and delivered the brakes by the deadline. With it, they sent a qualification report to show that the brake had passed the required ground tests and was ready for flight-testing.

However, during the flight tests several dangerous situations arose, and it became clear that the brake fell a long way short of requirements.

The OEM made several inquiries to AW&B before finally demanding to inspect the original test data. When they were at last allowed to see it, they discovered significant discrepancies between the qualification report and the data.

Humiliated, AW&B withdrew their brake system along with the report, and a number of engineers resigned. AW&B took another loss and had to offer an improved brake at the same price. They also launched an internal inquiry.

During the inquiry, managers and engineers seemed to be talking about two different worlds. Engineers told stories about professional training, specialist engineering expertise and experience in performing engineering tasks. They talked about set procedures, precision measurement and exact calculations. The data and calculations were viewed as either right or wrong; there was nothing in between.

In contrast, managers spoke about practical experience and length of service. They spoke of the 'big picture' in terms of community employment, order books, long-term survival and their own ability to understand strategic issues and make 'judgment calls'. Engineering data were looked on as needing to be interpreted to bring out the big picture.

	According to ENGINEERS...	According to MANAGERS...
ENGINEERS...	Are precise, deal in technical calculations, use technical criteria, have technical competence, judge success in terms of solving technical problems	Are nitpicking, can't grasp strategic issues, are upstarts, present conflicting data, are out of touch with the commercial world
MANAGERS...	Fudge, are bureaucratic, lie, prioritise money over being correct, are expedient	See the big picture, think strategically, prioritise the health of the business, interpret data, make judgment calls

Figure 10.1 Deadly embrace of Us and Them in the Aircraft Wheels & Brakes case

Figure 10.1 shows how the themes used by the managers and engineers relate. The two groups talk in very different terms about the 'brake scandal' and about each other. But notice that the themes interlock. In each case, what one side framed as good the other framed as bad. This creates a kind of deadly embrace of *Us and Them*.

As long as each side sees the other in the limited ways they do, they are caught in a trap with no clear options for escape. In fact whatever ideas they come up with are likely to reinforce perceptions rather than ease them. For example, if managers fired the 'guilty' engineers and tightened up procedures, that would just be seen as further bureaucracy, expedience and fudging. That's just a recipe for resistance.

Exercise
Caricatures

----

1 Identify *Us and Them* groups who are having trouble working together for the benefit of the company.
2 Caricature *Them*, and get their caricature of *Us*.
3 Notice how these caricatures restrict the possibilities of escape.
4 Look for individual members of the other group who are exceptions in some way to the caricature (recall the Total Person Inventory exercise above).
5 What new conversations could unlock the problem?
6 Bring both groups together to look at the caricatures and exceptions. Ask, 'How can we release the deadly embrace by relating in new ways?'

Working with the *Us and Them* Dynamic

In truth, you can only control the *Us and Them* dynamic up to a point. After all, *They* have a large measure of autonomy. If you try to control them by restricting that autonomy, you'll get all that resistance to change that we hear about. To a large degree in fact, would-be change agents create resistance to change.

A first step is to simply recognise that *Us and Them* dynamics are a primary factor in organisations. I don't find they are an explicit topic for senior managers, but it pays to be sensitive to them. Let's look at a range of ways to work with your *Us and Them* dynamics. If you like the slogan 'culture eats strategy for breakfast' (which I think was originally coined by Henry Mintzberg) then I think you can see how this is going to pay off.

Category	Action	Message received	Beneficial, harmful or neutral to your purposes?
Responses to reports of regulatory violations	Whistleblowers are sacked	*They* (management) are just paying lip service to the rules	Harmful
Engagement	President does a night shift from time to time	He's down to earth, respects the work – he's one of *Us*.	Beneficial
Executive perks	Executive dining rooms	*They* make sure their nests are feathered	Harmful or neutral depending on perceived legitimacy

Figure 10.2 Make an inventory of the messages people are getting

1. Recognise that you are always redefining *Us and Them*

As the communications theorists say: 'You cannot not communicate.' That means you are actively shaping the *Us and Them* dynamics every day. Figure 10.2 provides a few examples.

It's a useful exercise to think about how you would continue this list using examples from your own organisation.

2. Build up enriched pictures of groups and relationships

Figure 10.3 represents an organisational context in the form of a Rich Picture (a term coined by its originator, Peter Checkland).

Some conventions to note: individual and groups are represented as 'stick people'. Their concerns and objectives are captured in thought-bubbles. Lines of alliance or conflict are labelled with smiles or crossed swords as appropriate. Influential observers (media,

Principle Eight: Look Beyond 'Us and Them'

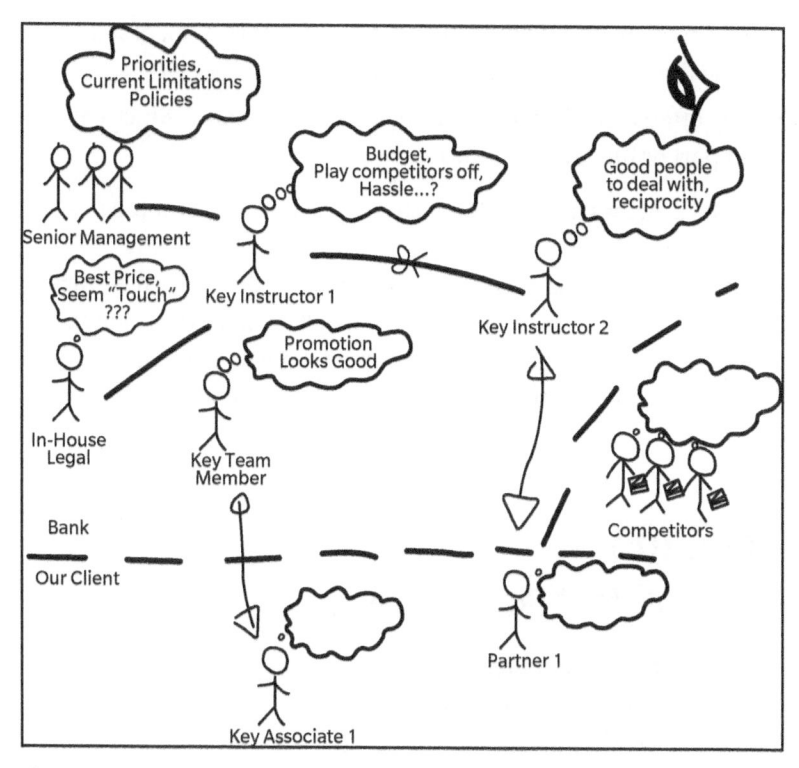

Figure 10.3 Rich Picture of a bank's legal department (from *Networkability: Building Your Business One Relationship at a Time*, by Helga Henry and Andy Bass, reproduced with permission)

regulatory authorities, etc.) are shown by eyeballs. Beyond these basics, you are free to make up further icons as you go.

As simple as this seems, the effect of a Rich Picture can be dramatic. I find that Rich Pictures have a number of benefits:

- they enable us to step back from, and out of, the detail of a situation, boosting objectivity and taking out emotion;
- they allow the identification of the multiple, often incompatible mindsets among which any solution is going to have to be an accommodation;
- they represent story themes simultaneously rather sequentially, helping to reduce any bias created by whose story we heard first;

- they break up the story elements so our memory bank of stereotypical stories is less likely to be triggered;
- they often identify surprising networks of influence which can support or hinder your efforts.

Box 10.1 provides prompts for ensuring you develop a thorough – rich – view.

On a number of occasions it's taken no more than a Rich Picture for a team of directors simply to say to me: 'Oh, okay, the solution is now obvious.' And even when that doesn't happen, the resulting discussion and investigation are always penetrating and insightful.

Box 10.1
Prompts for a Rich Picture

Stakeholders and Roles ...
    Who is actually in the organisation?
    Who does the work?
    Who sets goals?
    Who does the organisation interact with outside its boundary (customers, suppliers, influencers)?
    Who is watching the organisation?

Cultural Values, Norms, Worldviews
    What do people act to gain and keep?
    Slogans?
    Metaphors?
    Distinctive ways of acting?
    Contradictions (e.g. says one thing and does another)?
    What topics have to be addressed with sensitivity?

Power and Politics ...
    Who has authority over whom?
    Are there conflicting interests or a lack of cooperation?
    Who controls resources?
    Who controls environmental constraints (e.g. Regulatory)?

Case study
Ending a strategic deadlock and paving the way for a lucrative trade sale

A Rich Picture was pivotal in work I did with the deadlocked board of an international financial services business. Four directors held 20% each, with the remaining shares split between a small group of senior managers. The directors needed to agree a new strategic direction, and to gain committed support from staff and management.

For many years, they had worked on the settlement of reinsurance claims arising from the use of hazardous building materials. It had been a massive stream of work. But now, the majority of claims had been settled, and there were no new cases because the materials in question had been banned. The work was drying up. While they had huge technical skills and a top-flight reputation, they had limited sales capability. They would now need to find many individually smaller projects on which to work, and frankly they weren't sure they could.

There were various views about what to do. One director wanted to try to put the business on a new entrepreneurial growth footing. Another wanted to accept a modest offer to be acquired by a trade buyer rather than risk the business 'withering on the vine'. Another had been offered a partnership at a Big Four accountancy firm, and while he didn't want to leave his colleagues in the lurch, he was concerned about paying his kids' university fees. The minority shareholders felt excluded from the process. There was a lot of *Us and Them* going on, straining old friendships to near breaking point.

I interviewed everyone and produced a composite rich picture. When I showed it to the directors on a screen, something jumped out at me.

'You each think the others are being obdurate. But actually you're all behaving completely reasonably, if you consider when you each need money, and your personal risk preferences.'

The whole dynamic changed in an instant. Actually, they realised, no one person was to blame – the problem was the interaction among them.

Once they realised that they were still on the same side, it was plain sailing. We were quickly able to fashion a direction that attracted all the needed buy-in. The new strategy involved shuffling their portfolio of business in order to maintain and enhance top-line growth, as well as gaining acceptance of greater flexibility of staffing assignments to increase utilisation. They also recognised the hidden sales asset represented by their excellent relationships in the market. The resulting strengthened business was snapped up on very agreeable terms by a plc buyer within 12 months. All the directors and managers got bigger and better jobs in the larger group.

3. Cross-pollinate tribes

A Rich Picture is a great way to prepare for a strategy of *cross-pollination*.[2] When you cross-pollinate, you put people from each camp into the other camp, with the aim of breaking down the tribes and creating a community.

As well as taking a look at animosities (the crossed swords in your Rich Picture), you also want to look for the commonalities. In reality people in different silos usually have more in common than they think – not least a common interest that the business thrives. You then take the formal and informal influencers and set them up as exemplars. That means making sure that people who act in accordance with the new community ethos are visible, and visibly prosper. Others will then see that emulating their behaviour is the way to advance in the company.

4. Choose organisational interventions which don't objectify *Them*

Many standard organisational interventions create unhelpful relationships, even when they're trying to help. For example, most businesses conduct employee surveys and focus groups. They can be useful, but if you're not careful, they objectify the employees by saying in effect: 'We are going to turn *Them* into an object of study.' The proof that this is less than engaging? Look at the effort managers go to get people to fill in the surveys.

In one shared services centre, part of a global investment bank I was working with, the COO was determined to have the highest response rate to the annual employee survey of all the bank's offices. He bribed, cajoled and exhorted his teams to complete the survey. And he won, achieving a 90%+ response rate, higher than any other centre. As you've guessed, the actual responses were almost universally damning (which is why the feedback sessions were delayed for months!).

Rather than treating employees like lab rats, there are other ways to involve them and create a much better relationship dynamic. These more enlightened methods can also have the advantage of compressing the whole information gathering, processing and responding processes into a massively parallel exercise over a highly compressed time period.

Here's an easy way to do just that, called Open Space.[3] It's traditionally done in large in-person groups, but my colleagues and I found we could adapt it to the online environment during the COVID-19 lockdown – indeed it was a useful source of employee engagement during that time.

Open Space is one of a bunch of ways to hold a self-organising large group meeting to address an issue of importance to all the participants. The issue, or focal question, might be something like: 'How do we improve cross-functional collaboration?', 'How do we accelerate product launches?', 'How do we improve materials flow through the facility?' or 'How do we give clients a seamless service in different geographies?'

In contrast to most meetings, awaydays and retreats, the agenda is not imposed by the organisers, but is determined 'live' by the participants – those people who are close to the daily action. Information gathering, decision-making and response planning happen in one event – far faster than the slow decision-making cycle of a survey-based approach. Box 10.2 outlines a typical briefing for an Open Space event. Notice how the inclusive language avoids sharpening any distinction between *Us and Them*.

I've used Open Space events to engage a wide variety of my clients' *Them* – factory workforces, university academics, community stakeholders, country-level managers at annual off-sites. We've enjoyed fast tangible improvements in, respectively, safety and on-time delivery, innovation in teaching, community regeneration and strategic buy-in.

In my experience, the key to success with this approach is the attitude of the leader who sponsors it. Open Space can dissolve the sense of *Us and Them*, and leaders have to be prepared for that. The difficulty sometimes is that the leader might still be trying to preserve the illusion that they must come up with all the answers.

Box 10.2
Briefing an Open Space event

- We are here to address... (the focal question).
- We as a group will determine the agenda, and we may adjust it as we go.
- If you want, you can now decide to run a session on a topic you believe relevant to our focal question.
- In the centre of the room you will see pens and paper.
- Make a sign-up sheet and announce the topic, time and location of your session.
- Place the sign-up sheet on the wall in the relevant slot.
- You host the session and are responsible for producing a session report.
- Anyone can go to any session – please sign upon the sheets on the wall.
- Hosts, please post your session reports after the session.
- We will revisit the agenda during the day.

If you will just give permission, space and some sponsorship – including a modicum of inexpensive resources – *They* could do wonders for you and your business.

5. Don't impose 'solutions' on *Them*: enable people to solve their own problems

Very often the easiest way to improve performance is to get the people you are trying to engage to do it for you, or actually, to do it for themselves.

At one financial institution I worked with, employee satisfaction among new recruits was embarrassing, and staff turnover was proving costly. Employees felt like cogs in a machine. They didn't understand how their jobs fitted in, or why they mattered. Attrition was high, and performance was sluggish. This was despite the extensive training materials and courses the company provided during induction to try to explain the job and its significance.

In response to the problem, the company engaged consultants to redesign the induction programme, but to no avail. Secretly pleased at the consultants' failure, corporate HR also tried a redesign, but again it made no difference.

The solution was as simple as convening teams of recent recruits – under the leadership of junior managers – and having them design their own induction programme.

The most successful team developed an interactive board game, in which players followed the journey of a financial trade through its various stages, getting clues from established colleagues running the actual desks involved. Some of these desks were in the same building and could be visited physically. Others necessitated international phone calls. The players raced each other to complete the process. By the time they had finished the game – win or lose – they had grasped the end-to-end process and started to build the relationships they would need across the business.

The solution was far more creative, effective and cheap than senior managers expected, and when the CEO saw it on his next visit, he immediately sponsored its global roll-out including spending a small amount to have the game materials professionally made.

Another of the ideas the team came up with was to build a website and post video interviews with staff at varying levels in the organisation. As the recruits interviewed the senior managers, they also broadened out their picture of the same managers.

Notice that I'm not suggesting games and websites as a general solution to staff induction problems. A key point of Chapter 9 was that there might be no *general* solutions to superficially similar organisational issues. Instead, the idea is that specific situations require specific solutions, and to find those solutions, it's well worth letting your people have a crack at sorting things out for themselves.

6. Rather than dissolving Us and Them, reframe it

On occasion, you can make use of the *Us and Them* dynamic, rather than attempting to dissolve it. One of my colleagues was once asked to improve the safety of a large petrol distribution centre that had experienced a catastrophic event. This was something that happened from time to time and the company's standard response each time was to add to the rulebook, hoping to plug the loopholes and compel safer behaviour with more regulations. The main effect, however, was to undermine management–workforce relations. The union saw the thicker rulebook as a message from management that accidents were the fault of the workers. Yet, the union complained: management expected more and faster performance in its schedules and incentives, which made the safety demands of the rulebook impossible to achieve in practice.

Clearly, a heavy-handed approach to rule enforcement was becoming counter-productive.

Recognising the conflicts of beliefs, a standard organisational development approach might have been to try to negotiate better relationships on the basis of shared interests and values. But at this point, trust was so low that the idea of values workshops and posters was about as credible as having managers and operators sitting in a circle, holding hands and singing 'Kumbaya'.

In a fuel depot, the more unsafe acts (for example, not earthing a truck before delivering fuel), the more frequent the catastrophe. My colleague recommended a way to reduce the number and frequency of unsafe acts by working *with* the existing rules, and with the existing relationship between union and management.

He suggested adding this single proviso to the rulebook: *Every unsafe act that is reported to management indemnifies the worker from disciplinary consequences.* So, if you see your union brother do something unsafe, you can keep management off his back by reporting it. But, crucially, if unreported unsafe acts are discovered, those involved will be disciplined (legitimately in the eyes of all) in order to keep the workforce safe.

In response, union members noticed unsafe acts and chastised one another for putting them all at risk while protecting them from disciplinary action by reporting the incident. Now, many more eyes were on the problem, and management had reliable data with which to determine safety hotspots and devise permanent fixes. Notice that it was not necessary or even particularly desirable to try to convince the workers to change their beliefs about the bosses.

Exercise
Looking at behaviour with fresh eyes

Train yourself to ask these two questions when faced with undesired behaviour patterns:

1 Ask: 'In what circumstance would this undesired behaviour actually be useful?' *For example, rumour-mongers can often provide a useful channel for internal communications.*

2 Ask: 'In what circumstances is the behaviour we want the natural response?' *For example, look how COVID-19 immediately precipitated widespread adoption of internet video conferencing (Zoom, Skype etc.). Many of my clients had been trying to get people to buy into that for years.*

What about *Customers*?

After having lost what should have been an easy case due to the unreliable evidence provided to the court by his own client, John Mortimer's fictional barrister Rumpole of the Bailey remarked wryly, 'Sometimes it would be a lot easier to be a lawyer if it wasn't for one's damned clients.'

Perhaps we've all had occasion to feel sympathy. The customer is *not* always right, whatever the cliché asserts to the contrary. That said, I've found we generally get the kinds of clients and customers we expect. Our *Us and Them* stories about our relationships with customers are therefore pivotal to business success. It is to this subject that we turn in the next chapter.

Chapter 11

Principle Nine: Bring Customers Inside

What Is in the Centre of Your Business's 'Map of the World?'

In mid-May 2016, I was in Amsterdam with colleagues from around the world. It was shortly before the referendum on the UK's membership of the European Union. Although we – like the pundits – were expecting a 'Remain' vote at this point, they teased me that on my next visit to the Netherlands, I would need a visa. They rather rudely bantered to the effect that they doubted my chances of being admitted to the country!

And one of them went further: 'Britain has to get used to the fact that it doesn't rule the world anymore.'

I countered that the Dutch have the same problem: while historical British Empire maps of the world centre on London, Dutch Empire maps quite naturally centre on Amsterdam! A Brazilian at the meeting laughed and said that he grew up with the Americas in the centre of the map.

The thing in the centre of the map is the thing we think is most important. Maps from old empires offer a limited viewpoint for navigating the world of today. So here's a question: What is in the centre of your business's 'map of the world?'

My bet is that the company is in the centre. Or maybe if we delved deeper we'd find a range of perspectives. It would turn out that there were various functions – finance, marketing, operations, IT, R&D, sales, HR and so on – each perceiving the world as if they are at its centre.

Fewer organisations really place the most important element of their business at the centre. I mean, of course, the customer. Ensuring the customer is at the centre is one of the most important and powerful things you can do as a business leader. There are many ways to do it. For example, you can:

- Immerse yourself in a customer-eyed view. If you can, shop at your own business. Call your own helpline. Order something. If you can't do it yourself, get someone you trust to do it. (I know this sounds like mystery shopping – it is, but the difference is that mystery-shopping programmes are often filtered before they reach the leader who can really influence things. I'm suggesting you go and see for yourself.)
- Do some customer journey mapping. It often throws up insights that make a big difference, and it's easy to do (some people inevitably try to make it complicated, but frankly there are plenty of YouTube videos explaining how to do it well enough to get results).

Or you can follow the approach of this chapter and bring customers inside.

It's Natural to Think about Customers as Being Outside

Most companies talk a good game about being customer-centric, but even the best ones perform patchily. Sure their sales and marketing, innovation and – one would hope but not bet – service functions might focus on customers. But R&D departments are sometimes more interested in technology than people. Operations might see customers as more of a hindrance than *raison d'etre*. And there are many people working in finance and HR who have never met a customer.

The customer-centric leader has to deal with the fact that it's natural for employees to think of customers as being 'outside' the business. After all, in physical terms, customers don't live in your buildings[1] (they come into retail outlets of course, but only as visitors from the outside, and they rarely show up at head office, the call centre or the factory). Significant numbers of employees, regardless of level, rarely if ever meet a customer in person. To the extent that customer-facing staff get replaced by chatbots, this will become even more true.

Customers: Us or Them?

In the previous chapter (Looking beyond *Us and Them*) we saw how thinking of other people as *Them* limits the ways we interact and locks us into oppositional patterns. If we see *Them* in the terms of a limited story, we miss potential. If we can step outside those limits, valuable solutions can open up.

There are many limiting ways businesses can think of customers. Box 11.1 provides some examples.

The clearest and most egregious modern case of a schism between a business and its customers is provided by the case of Boeing. Boeing executives and engineers knowingly did things – and failed to do other things – that made the 737 MAX aircraft a death trap. What's most amazing is that this was despite the fact that they themselves, and their loved ones, were highly likely to be 737 MAX passengers.

Who is the call centre for?

A far less dramatic but more often-encountered example of disconnection from customers is provided by call centres. You can immediately tell when a call centre is designed from a point of view that places the customer outside the business.

> **Box 11.1**
>
> **Limiting attitudes to customers**
>
> *Spoken idea – acceptable to say*
> - Conceding that while customers pay the bills, they are demanding
>
> *Unspoken idea – only to be shared with friends*
> - Joking that it would be easier to run the business without them!
>
> *Unconscious ideas – not OK to say, even to self*
> - Creating a false *Us and Them*, missing the fact that we are also customers
> - Projecting our organisation's failings on *Them*
> - Resenting the customer because the business needs them and so we might have to dance to their tune
> - Following the path of least resistance – wanting to do just enough to get paid

I overhead my friend's daughter calling a bus company about their timetable. The website was ambiguous, so she called the 'helpline' number displayed there. She was 'greeted' by the customary robotic 'Welcome to Acme Bus Company... we now have two options for you.' A few key presses later, she got through to an operator and asked for the bus times she needed.

'You've come through to the Midlands team. You need the South East team. I'll put you through.'

Before she could speak she was cut off and placed into a queue: five minutes of uninterrupted ringtone followed.

In frustration she hung up and called back, but it was Groundhog Day all over again: 'Welcome to Acme Bus Company... we now have two options for you.'

She pressed the key sequence and again reached an operator and asked for help.

Again: 'You've come through to the Midland team. You need the South East team. I'll put you through. . . '.

'NO WAIT!! Don't transfer me! That just happened and I spent five minutes listening to a ringtone wondering if anyone would ever answer. Can't you just tell me the time of my bus?'

'Oh, well the South East team (another disconnected *Them*, notice) were probably busy. They're in the same office (as *Us*) – I can see they are all on the phones.'

Huh?

Why does the bus company need regional teams when the timetable is on a computer network and they are all in the same office? Why do they transfer people into long call queues when they are sitting next to each other? Why don't they just handle the query? Is local knowledge so crucial?

Clearly this was organised to suit the internal convenience of the business, an internal world that did not include the customer.

Exercise
Your best and worst experiences as a customer

This simple and effective exercise is a great one to do with people at all levels within the organisation. Think of what it's like to be a customer. In particular, identify best and worst examples.

Example	How did it start?	How did it proceed?	How did it conclude?	Lessons you can apply
Your best experience as a customer				
Your worst experience as a customer				

When the Customer Is Part of the Business

Bringing the customer inside is a hugely underutilised approach in many companies. But some companies go to great lengths to bring consumers inside, and gain insights for new growth and productivity that are otherwise invisible to internal people.

Co-creating value with customers

McCain Foods faced a tough innovation challenge: how do you come up with anything new in the area of 'frozen products made of potato that you can buy in a supermarket'? On the face of it, this was not an area ripe for new ideas. Internal people thought they knew all the angles in this business and weren't particularly open to hearing anything new. It wasn't arrogance, they just didn't think there was anything new to hear. Aided by, among others, my colleague Jack Martin Leith, McCain held Open Space meetings with consumers (see Chapter 10). The wrinkle was that they invited key internal people to attend as 'witnesses'. To their surprise, the witnesses gained all kinds of insights about how their products were viewed, and they came up with a range of new ideas, two of which became high-selling profitable new products for McCain. Some of the most resistant internal people were highly enthused by the approach and became vociferous champions for these new initiatives. We've had fantastic results using similar approaches in both B2B and B2C situations.

How Lego turned a talent problem on its head

LEGO went even further than inviting customers inside, and actually *recruited* customers, thereby fixing a fundamental problem. Previously the company had gone to great lengths to hire the best designers it could find. And being LEGO, they had access to some very good designers indeed. The problem was, as good as they were at design, these people didn't 'get' LEGO. They designed brilliant things that LEGO users weren't interested in.

Then the company realised something: they had an underappreciated resource in the shape of a sophisticated adult user community. They turned the problem on its head: maybe some members of the adult user community happened to be designers? Some were, and they were recruited, designing winning products.

More Ways to Bring Customers Inside

Your customers know more about what they will buy than you do. How can you get them to share that knowledge as widely as possible in your company?

1. Invite your customers' decision-makers to talk to your staff

This is very easy, and most businesses in my experience should do more of it. Customers are often delighted to be invited to speak to their suppliers' staff. Bring them into Town Hall meetings or invite them on site visits. If they can't attend in person, see if you can get them to speak on video. There are many benefits:

- Customers' messages on the importance of quality, on-time delivery and service are more credible than those of managers because they are not seen as having any ulterior motive such as boosting their bonuses.
- Employees love to see that their efforts are appreciated by customers – most typically go without such feedback (and even taking the boss's word for it is never as compelling as hearing it direct from the customer).

- Customers really enjoy it – it's a high compliment that you value their opinion so much, and it will strengthen the relationship.
- You will get the chance to talk to your customers informally while arranging and hosting their visits, thereby gaining valuable insights you might otherwise have missed.

2. Deconstruct client testimonials

Asking for testimonials is invaluable for marketing, of course. But there's another less obvious benefit: you may be surprised to find that you are more valuable to your customers than you think!

The great thing about this surprise value is that you can build on the evidence of what works to make your business even more attractive to customers. You can discover new growth opportunities with a high probability of success.

For example, recently I noticed a pattern in testimonials from my own advisory clients. The surprise value was this: I was giving them the support and encouragement to stick to their guns.

One leader said I helped her and her board, 'hold the strategic line when everything around us was going nuts'. Another client, the founder of a marketing agency, said I helped his business, 'fulfil its potential without succumbing to pressure to compromise the vision'. He said a big part of that was about holding the line on fees commensurate with their premium positioning. He went on to suggest that this kind of advice was ideal for people who don't want their vision to 'get lost, derailed, or diluted along the way'.

I hadn't recognised that this aspect of my work was something that people were valuing. But since then I've started to emphasise it when it's been relevant to prospective advisory clients.

Exercise
Using testimonials to find hidden value

1 Assemble a set of testimonials.

2 First, look for common patterns that tell you something new – It can help to find an objective third party to help you look with fresh eyes. Can you find any surprise value of the sort we discussed above? For example, look for

- descriptions of benefits that are different from those you describe in your marketing materials and
- examples of your people going above and beyond expectations.

For an objective view that might detect things you miss, get someone like a good marketing copywriter to review the testimonials for you.

3 Next, think back to Chapter 5 (Reverse engineer yourself). Are the testimonials pointing you to implicit resources that you could make overt and rebundle to provide a new engine of growth?

3. Create deep conversations and listen closely

Henry Ford is famously supposed to have said: 'If I'd asked people what they wanted, they'd have said "a faster horse"'. (It's doubtful that he did say this by the way, but in these days of fake news many would regard it as 'a story that's too good to check'.)

Even if it's apocryphal, the 'faster horse' quote offers a couple of instructive lessons. Most often, it is taken as evidence that customers struggle to articulate what they want, so it's no good asking them. You'll just get incremental ideas that make little difference: a faster horse, a thinner smartphone, that sort of thing. This observation has some truth to it, and if it encourages people to prototype ideas and observe people's behaviour in real-world settings, then that's a good thing.

However, there's a second, equally important lesson. Even if customers can't give you radical new ideas, they can provide something very valuable if you know what you're listening for: insights.

A faster horse isn't much of an idea if the alternative is a car. But forget about the word 'horse'. The word to pay attention to is 'faster'. Here is where the potential insight is. To turn that potential insight into a real one, just ask every three-year-old's favourite question: 'WHY?'

(Why faster?)

The answer will depend on the respondent:

> 'Well (assuming 1908 work practices and technology), I want it to be faster because then I can get to town for my groceries and be back to work on the farm more quickly.'

Or they might say:

> 'Well, I run a messenger service and people want replies to their letters more quickly. If I could increase the speed of my service, I'd get a great advantage over my competitors.'

Now we have not just a low-grade idea but some potentially golden insights! In both cases, armed with the insight we might come up with a bunch of genuinely good ideas (cars, telephones, grocery delivery services) to better meet the customer's needs.

How do you go about systematically finding such insights? There are many ways, but a good way to start is to create entirely novel conversations between people who don't usually talk (e.g. between infrequent customers and employees who don't get out much).

You also have to make sure that you can really listen to and hear things that challenge 'what everybody knows' about how your industry works.

4. Change the way you label the relationship

Very few lawyers talk about having customers; they have clients. Psychotherapists also tend to refer to the people they see as clients, while psychiatrists see them as patients. Academics often resist attempts to characterise students as customers, even though those students may be paying considerable fees. Why do people care about these labels? Because the language people use to describe the person who pays the bill carries unspoken assumptions about the relationship.

Some businesses have created valuable advantages by finding new ways to frame relationships. The following table shows some examples.

Customer outside	Customer inside
Credit card customer	Member (e.g. Amex)
Consultancy client	Associate Member of Think-tank (e.g. Interchange Research)
Equity investor	Limited partner (Private equity)

Can you do something similar? It's worth exploring with your 'customers'.

This idea needs a caveat. Of course you could change the language and hope to influence people to buy the same old wine in a new bottle. But to do that risks warranted scepticism from intelligent customers. To make this work, you actually have to rethink the relationship in line with the new label, creating uniqueness and new value for all parties.

5. Make the customer the hero of the story

One of the first pieces of advice given to beginning marketing copywriters is to make liberal use of the word *You* in their copy. In contrast – as a cursory inspection of a few company websites will show you – many businesses lead with a lot of talk of *We*. These businesses fall into the trap of talking about themselves too much. They emphasise their company's proud history, achievements, technology and certifications. The way they frame their marketing places the customer outside the business.

Why do businesses so often default to talking about themselves? Most likely they're simply reflecting what they focus on day-to-day: their own expertise, processes and goals. And to be completely fair, they also have the legitimate need to establish credibility. It's a tricky balance to strike, which is one reason why good copywriters are well compensated.

Here's a helpful way to rebalance. Ask yourself and your team, 'Who's the hero? Our business, or our customer?' The answer will usually be the customer. After all, as Don Miller points out, they are the central character in their own story. It's understandable that they will cast your business in a supporting role, however important.

While accepting that idea to some degree, you may still wonder, 'If they are the hero, and if our messages are all about them, how *do* we convey our value, our expertise, know-how and credibility?'

One answer is by playing your supporting role powerfully: for example as their mentor, or their guide, or their ally.[2] You might think of yourself as the Obi Wan to their Luke, the Morpheus to their Neo, or the Good Witch to their Dorothy. This archetypal way of thinking cements the hero's – that is, the customer's – position in the centre of the action. And crucially, it does so without downplaying the mentor's credibility and prestige.

Think about how archetypal mentors connect with their sometimes reluctant mentees. They are challenging, surprising, confident, fascinating and balanced. They are often more ambitious for their mentees than their mentees are for themselves. And they know they have to establish their credibility through *demonstrations* not just words. Not a bad set of qualities to reflect in your relationships with your customers.

Taking customer relationships beyond *Us and Them*

Douglas Wright Restaurants is a leading UK franchisee of McDonald's. Starting from one restaurant in 2002, Doug and his team have grown the business to a turnover of more than £50M with 20 locations and around 2000 staff. In a business renowned for its obsession with process, they have pioneered flexible employment policies that have been vital for growth while still delivering the consistency for which McDonald's is globally famous.

Doug epitomises the idea of bringing customers inside. He is clear that his customers – and the communities they live in – are often his staff as well.

Doug identifies a key challenge faced by many businesses as 'localising a global brand'. That means being embedded in the local community, so that customers, employees and prospective employees see beyond a faceless corporate entity to the real people behind the brand. Doing that requires balancing the discipline of process with the human touch.

They didn't start this way. In the early days, Doug and his team ran the business 'in a regimented way, with military precision'. They did everything by the book (that is to say, the McDonald's Employee Handbook). But the team soon realised that in their locale, 'by the book' wasn't giving them the commitment they needed from people. So they stood their approach on its head and resolved to go out of their way to make things work for each individual based on their unique needs. 'Maximum flexibility' became their mantra.

As Doug explains: 'Rather than telling an employee "The handbook says NO", we asked ourselves, "How can we say YES?"'

He goes on, 'If someone can only work four days or limited hours because of commitments as a carer, or wants indefinite maternity leave, or even to take a year off to travel, if they're committed to us, we'll make it work. It's how we differentiate ourselves as an employer. We focus on retention over recruitment. We are constantly thinking about our talent pipeline so that we have people ready for promotion, or to staff new restaurants, before we need them. It's created huge loyalty among our people, not to mention vital trust in the local community.'

The idea of *bringing customers inside* is fundamental to Douglas Wright Restaurant's growth. Its pragmatism is further underlined by the successful turnaround of restaurants Doug's team has taken over from less successful operators.

Your Customers Know What Works

As we move through our lives both inside and outside our businesses, we are all variously customers, contributors and community members. Shifting our perspectives among these roles can be extremely valuable. But most people don't go about these perspective shifts deliberately.

We naturally place ourselves at the centre of our own maps and as the central characters in our own stories. But when it comes to relationships with customers, we can learn a lot by putting them in the centre.[3]

This is true regardless of how the business is performing now. Even a mediocre business – as long as it has customers – is doing some things that work. It can become a better business by starting there: engaging customers to find out what it's doing right, deepening its understanding of the resources that underpin any success it's having, and building on that to be more consistent.

And an excellent business, already enjoying superb customer relationships, can work with them to advance further, continuing to develop and capitalise on its unique resources to ensure it continues to thrive.

Chapter 12

Principle Ten: Give Control to Get Control

How long does it take for a radio signal to reach from the Earth to a Mars-roving robot? The answer is anything between 4 minutes and 22 minutes depending on the relative distances of the two planets. That means that if you want to control the Rover, you can't just treat it like a drone, hooking up a camera to the front and steering it using a game controller back at mission control.

Why? Because in the 8 to 44 minutes it takes for the signal to yo-yo to Mars and back, your precious Rover could already have driven over the edge of a cliff. In order to control the Rover you have to build up and rely upon its ability to sense and respond to its surroundings autonomously. In order to complete the mission, you have to give control to get control.

In the same way, if you want an organisation that is responsive to the market and to customers, you can't have every decision escalated to senior management. If you try that, you'll be outmanoeuvred by more agile competitors. You'll also create a sense of learned helplessness in your people. Nothing slows organisations down more than passivity and the waste of unnecessary waiting.

The lesson of the Mars Rover is especially useful when working with managers who consider themselves 'hardnosed'. These managers often resist ideas such as empowerment and inclusion. They think such concepts are 'touchy-feely' and idealistic. But the lesson of the Mars Rover has nothing to do with recognition of its robotic dignity. It's just the way the engineering has to be done.

Organisations that give control to get control reap the value of faster decision-making, closer to the action. In a world that is harder than ever to predict, that is a dependable advantage: customer issues are resolved more quickly, you can stay ahead of competitors, and projects spend less time spinning their wheels.

That said, devolution of control can go too far. The crucial issue for leaders is to balance autonomy and direct control.

Get This Done 'Somehow' or I'll Find Someone Who Can

In a Middle European country in the 1930s, so the story goes, the management of a gun factory were told by the newly installed communist government to stop manufacturing arms, but to continue to keep the factory open, and to continue paying the workers. When they enquired about how they were supposed to achieve this, the one-word answer that came back was: 'Somehow'.

Somehow Management is alive and well. It feels good to set a vision and then, like Jean-Luc Picard on the Starship Enterprise, say: 'Make it so.' And of course managers can claim that this constitutes delegation and empowerment – good things. But Picard is relying on a disciplined and highly trained crew with rigorous procedures worked out by rocket scientists. Even he can't mandate the impossible, or if he cares about morale, the unreasonable.

Management by objectives is a fine approach. But as political demagogues consistently demonstrate, setting forth visions and goals is not enough. Delegation is not abdication, and even if they can't do it all themselves, it's the responsibility of managers to ensure that:

- organisational plans, initiatives and structures add up to an adequate framework to achieve the strategic objectives they have set;
- said plans and initiatives are adequately resourced;
- there is sufficient slack and contingency available to cover inevitable bumps in the road;
- progress is tracked tightly enough and feedback loops are responsive enough to adjust if the plans and structures turn out, despite best intentions, to be wrong or inadequate.

There are plenty of tools to do this, and quite often, there are competent people on staff who know them but aren't listened to (granted sometimes these people are so inarticulate when discussing anything but methodology that they are their own worst enemies, but that is another story!).

It may feel like dynamic leadership, but it's lazy and ineffective management to set forth a dramatic vision or stretch goal, and then mandate its achievement 'somehow', abdicating responsibility for designing a credible implementation scheme.

Box 12.1
Somehow Management can wear a cynical mask

I once worked with a University with a highly dysfunctional organisational climate. The Vice-Chancellor (essentially the CEO) had created what he called an 'internal trading model'. The idea was that each department, whether an academic department or a support function, operated as a profit centre, had control of its own budget, and was freed from traditional requirements to use internal providers. So for example, the Business School could 'subcontract' teaching to the Psychology Department, and could either get printing done by the Reprographics Department, or go to an outside vendor such as Kall-Kwik. The advertised rationale for the trading model had

> two strands: (1) it exposed support functions such as Reprographics to external competition, which would drive up quality and increase value for money; (2) it gave leaders autonomy and a sense of self-determination.
>   Did it work? It's impossible to say, because the Vice-Chancellor covertly manipulated the market by dictating everybody's costs – apparently so that he could shut down service departments. His other motivation appeared to be that he could now offload blame for organisational performance shortfalls, saying, 'I've devolved responsibility to you. It's up to you to achieve results (somehow, even though I'm manipulating the market), so if you don't like the results you are getting, it's your fault.'

Under-determined methods and magical thinking – it'll work 'somehow'

'Somehow Management' is the idea that because you *will* something, or because you insist on it, or because it follows logically from your theory or ideology, that it will somehow – magically – come to pass. It's saying 'failure is not an option' when it's obvious that failure is very much an option, and a truly competent executive would be busy putting preventative and mitigating actions in place rather than relying on faith and affirmation.

As any BS artist knows (and as board directors should remember) you can go a long way by setting out a dramatic vision or list of stretch goals, and then mandating their achievement 'somehow', while abdicating responsibility for designing a credible implementation scheme – as long as you skip on to the next job before the reckoning. (Some people you can read about in the newspapers have ended up running public companies and even countries this way.)

Setting those more extreme examples to the side, how often do you see strategic plans comprising a 'compelling vision' and a huge raft of apparently corresponding KPIs, but no real link between them? They are like sandwiches without any jam.

Vision is vital, or else you just get uninspired, incremental strategies that are warmed over versions of what you said you'd do last year. But visions are not achieved 'somehow'.

Michelin's 'Responsabilisation' programme

The tyre manufacturer Michelin traditionally had an ethos of empowerment. But in the early 2000s it embraced the trend for the KPI-heavy centralised management systems being promulgated by large management consultancies. The growth of these approaches has been driven by the tendency to think of organisations mechanistically – they are looked at as if they are computers, and the humans working in them as if they are processing units. The problem for Michelin was that obsessing over top-down KPIs was stifling initiative and creativity. (Michelin's experience is far from unique. In another well-publicised example, 3M found its famously innovative culture undermined by the uber-standardisation of Six Sigma, and in Britain, the New Public Management movement created a backlash, as 'gaming' of KPIs produced unintended negative consequences.)

Managers at Michelin resolved to do something radically different to the KPI-heavy trend. Under the leadership of Jean-Dominique Senard, its CEO from 2012 to 2019, and continuing today, the company has dramatically increased the autonomy of frontline workers in a programme it calls Responsabilisation.[1]

Starting with experiments in a restricted number of plants, team leaders asked workers questions such as:

- 'What decisions could you make without my help?'
- 'What problems could you solve without the involvement of support staff like maintenance, quality or industrial engineering?'

Typical areas identified have included shift scheduling, and as people have gained more experience, aspects of production planning. Workers were given responsibility to run and improve these areas. The teams work within a framework, which includes the vision and values of the group and the behaviour expected of Michelin staff, as well as hard constraints such as availability of resources, along with legal and safety rules. They are also given support with resources and skills, and then given wide latitude to achieve results. Teams evaluate their own performance and liaise with other autonomous teams in the factory.

Team leaders are encouraged to step back and shift their role from 'deciding' to 'enabling'. They now act as coaches or, in the event of a disagreement, referees. As lessons have been learned, they have been spread around the company. Michelin estimates that the programme has added half a billion dollars' worth of improvements, and has created a culture of greater trust and commitment providing a platform for further gains.

Preserving the leader's intent

How does a leader ensure that their intent is preserved, while allowing their people the leeway necessary to enable them to achieve that intent? The most challenging arena for testing answers to this question is the military realm, and so this is a good place to look for solutions. And indeed people have always looked to military models of organisation for management ideas. However, there has been a huge shift in thinking about military organisation that is not necessarily reflected in the structures and practices of many businesses.

Many people in corporations have an outmoded idea of what today's military strategists regard as effective methods of command. The traditional hierarchical view of command and control sees orders cascading down a chain of middle management from the top. It reached its zenith in the Pyrrhic waste of WW1 attrition warfare – hardly an ennobling model for efficient deployment of resources in a fast-changing environment.

As they say in the military: 'No plan survives first contact.' People on the ground need to make decisions according to the circumstances of the moment, rather than being constrained by robotic scripts and fixed procedures like so many hapless call centre operators. As we've seen, a Mars Rover, which is a real robot, has to be given enough autonomy and trust to make steering decisions when it starts roving on the planet.

Colonel Boyd and 'The Mission Contract'

We first met the influential strategist, USAF Colonel and fighter ace John R. Boyd in Chapter 8. Boyd noted that throughout history smaller military organisations have been able to prevail over larger and stronger opponents when they found ways to preserve the commander's intent while devolving as much tactical decision-making as possible to the people at the sharp end of any action.

Beyond his influence in the military sphere, Boyd's work has influenced a number of business thinkers, notably Tom Peters. Boyd himself was an enthusiastic student of the Toyota Production System, which he saw as an (independently developed) business example of the same principles underlying his own theory. Promotion of Boyd's work is continued by his acolytes, and the leading figure in the translation of his ideas into the business world is Chet Richards, who among other concepts discusses the mission contract, an invaluable framework for delegation-without-abdication.

A mission contract involves an explicit transfer of ownership of responsibility for results. Here is a template for delegating by negotiating a mission contract, with acknowledgement to the influence of Colonel Boyd and Dr Richards. I've used this template very successfully with coaching clients, both new leaders fighting a tendency to micromanage and experienced ones swamped by the attempts of their reports to 'delegate upwards'.

REWARDS format for mission delegation

If leaders can't delegate a job to someone else and get it returned to a required standard, then they can't build leverage. Without leverage, productive capacity is going to be limited by the number of hours a leader can work personally.

In the words of General George Patton: 'Don't tell people how to do things, tell them what to do and let them surprise you with their results.' As well as benefiting from their ingenuity, there's another plus: if you are too specific about the route to achieving a goal and there turn out to be unforeseen roadblocks, some subordinates will give up and dump it back at your door: 'You told me to go this way, and it didn't work, so I give up – over to you.' If you have specified the destination, not the route, then the onus remains on them to find their way – it's reasonable for them to consult with you and request extra help, but not to give up.

Here's a format that works very well, based on the British Army's 'Mission Command' process. I came up with the mnemonic 'REWARDS' to make it easy to remember:

R esults required
E vidence for success
W hy is the result important?
A gree to make a contract
R esources and support negotiation
D ocument the agreement
S upport the delegate

Here are the steps in more detail:

1 **Results.** Delegate the results you want, not the method. Hold people accountable for the result: not just for following the process or completing the checklist. Of course you should provide help, guidance, proven processes and tools, but keep making it clear that the job is to get the result, not just go through the motions.

2 **Evidence.** How will you both know for sure that you got the result? Here's a common, and very annoying problem: you ask someone to do something, and what you get is not what you wanted, but you can see how they got the wrong end of the stick. You end up settling for what you didn't want, or having the work

done over – a real nuisance. Usually the culprit is vague language. Make it absolutely clear what you want to see, hear and/or feel that will confirm the result. For example, 'What I am really after is a one page press release on my desk, with all the right facts and contact details already filled in, that makes the reader feel like they want to get on the phone for the story immediately'.

3 **Why?** Make it clear why the result is important at two levels of objective above. This is where our early discussion of *distilled essence* comes in (Chapter 9: Use very plain words). Individual jobs, especially staff jobs, can seem quite disconnected from the world of living, breathing customers. Explain how the result you are requesting contributes to the mission of the business. It helps people get motivated, it shows how your request is reasonable, and it enables them to improvise if they come up against problems.

4 **Agree.** Make it plain that you are proposing a contract, or agreement – ask them if they accept. You can coerce people to do things, but that's not delegation. Instead, you ask them: 'Are you prepared to sign up to this? If you do, you are accountable.' Be vigilant that they don't accept too automatically. Consider playing devil's advocate. Maybe they ought to go and do some research before they commit themselves. If they are more junior, this is a big opportunity to coach and develop them.

5 **Resources and constraints.** Allow the assignee to negotiate changes to the specification, including resources, support and ground rules. Ideally you want someone who says 'Yes, I can make this happen for you, as long as I have the following resources'. The negotiation process is crucial for creating commitment (this is the process inherent in transferring ownership of the job).

6 **Document** the agreement. A simple email will be enough in some cases. In others, something more akin to a project proposal, with milestones, metrics, etc. will be needed. Your decision about appropriate documentation will be a function of a number of things, including your level of trust in their competence to deliver.

7 **Support** and monitor, but don't solve all their problems for them. There's a difference between delegation and abdication.
8 On completion, acknowledge results and give out **REWARDS**. This doesn't have to be a big deal, but it shouldn't be skipped either. Since real motivation is intrinsic, the best reward comes from helping someone feel personal satisfaction and an increasing sense of competence.

Set 'impossible but fun' challenges

Don't misinterpret my railing against Somehow Management to be counselling a lack of ambition. It makes sense to challenge people so that their ingenuity is released. We just don't want to then leave them high and dry. Somehow Management doesn't give them a *context* in which they can succeed. We want to create the context. A great way to do that is the 'impossible but fun' challenge. Rather than trying to reach some idea goal for evermore, what if you just tried to achieve the standard for one day, or one week?[2]

Here's the sort of situation that's great for an impossible but fun challenge. You want to achieve some ambitious daily, weekly or monthly performance level in some area of the business. It could be anything: zero defects, 100% schedule attainment, response to client enquiries within a certain time, quotes out within a certain time, or zero unsafe acts. Everyone acknowledges the importance of the goal, but in practice it is rarely if ever met, and if people were honest, they'd admit that they just can't see how to do it.

The idea of meeting such standards day in and day out can seem insurmountable if it's never been achieved before. But what if you made a game out of it?

In one manufacturing plant, Tom, the factory manager, was struggling with a common issue. When they were under time pressure to meet delivery promises people rushed, and quality suffered.

To address it, I suggested Tom organise a 'model day' experiment. He selected a day that was two weeks ahead and attached a simple goal to it: For one day, meet the aggressive schedule with zero defects. See if we can do it, and discover what we can learn from trying.

The exercise was a great success. As Tom explained:

'I used the REWARDS delegation format to brief everybody on what we were going to do (see Figure 12.1).

We actually tried it on two lines on two different days. We started by picking straight runs with no changeovers so that we had a good chance of success. It was great that everybody who was on the factory floor that day had a go – everybody rotated in and out of those lines. And at the end of the day they were running over to the whiteboards to find out: "Did we do it?"

It engaged people. Especially when I explained the "Whys": a lot of people had never been talked to like that. Previously, the attitude was: "If we don't get it done – oh well." They didn't understand the consequences. They appreciated having an explanation, and they appreciated knowing the results. Now I am picking lines with changeovers to make it more of a challenge, and we're going to make a video documentary so we can show it to teams in other plants.'

To set your own 'impossible but fun' challenge, follow these steps:

- Identify an ambitious performance level you want to achieve.
- Pick a date two or three weeks in the future on which you will aim to have a perfect 'model' day.
- Announce your intentions well in advance. Brief the relevant people using the REWARDS delegation formula.
- Record the preparations and the action on the day, using photos and videos.

- Hold an all-hands meeting afterwards to review lessons, and discuss how that level of performance can become the new business-as-usual standard.
- Set up the next challenge.

An App in a day!

Businesses large and small are having to get to grips with digitalisation. Deutsche Bank became very conscious that if digital transformation was to meet the real needs of customers and employees, it

R esults required   Hit at least 80% quality on line K throughout the day of 16th October.
E vidence for success   Visual management boards next to the line will show the performance. We will also film the line and the management boards during the day and display it on the TV monitors throughout the plant.
W hy is the result important? (2 levels)   We will learn a lot about how to improve quality and consistency on line K. We will minimise customer complaints.
A gree to make a contract   We want everyone on the team to agree to pursue this goal, so we've asked you to please tell us what you need.
R esources and support negotiation   We've agreed the following resources:
D egree of Documentation   This form documents the agreement. In addition, let's record the following joint accountabilities: I (factory manager) will: You (team) will: We will jointly:
S upport the delegate

Figure 12.1 Using the REWARDS format to set an 'impossible but fun' challenge

couldn't just be seen as the sole province of technologists. It's easy in any organisation for people to develop silo mindsets, but for digital transformation to really work, people from across the business need opportunities to participate in and contribute to areas that they may have shied away from in the past.

Deutsche Bank organised a 24-hour Hackathon in which small, multi-disciplinary teams competed to produce apps for the charity Autistica. The teams included not only technologists but people from around the business: trading, HR, legal, compliance etc. The winning app included an emotion diary to help young people with autism to understand and manage anxiety.

The bank followed the success of the Autistica Hackathon with a similar event for Cure Leukemia. The winning team developed a prototype app that suggests 'buddies' with similar diagnoses, age and gender. It also curates articles from trusted sources and keeps track of a patient's well-being and key statistics. Patients can choose to share this information with friends, family, buddies or doctors, as well as fetch blood test results and report their daily progress.

In addition to the intrinsic value of helping these great causes, there have been business benefits for the bank too. These include connecting people who wouldn't otherwise work together, underlining the value of being a DB employee – important for satisfaction and retention – and most importantly, broadening people's horizons, particularly by exposing them to digital technologies and methods such as Agile, which they are now applying to their own disciplines, e.g. HR.

Getting diverse teams together to work on a short-term, high-impact project for a meaningful cause provides a great way to develop your organisation's learning capacity, build relationships across the company and start to mitigate the effects of organisational silos. It is also a far more 'real' and lasting morale booster than can ever be provided by empty 'jollies' or motivational trainers.

Delegation and Motivation

The idea of *giving control to get control* relies on a different view of 'motivation' than the traditional one popular in leadership training. In short, I start from the position that *you can't motivate people*. That's because, in essence, they are already motivated. This goes for employees, peers, customers, and in fact for all human beings (and other living creatures).

Think of the laziest person you know. From one perspective they are solid blocks of inertia. But from another – more useful – one, they are highly motivated.

By what? By the desire to avoid hassle and discomfort, and to seek comfort and ease. If you want proof, try to get them to do something they don't want to do, and you will be met with energetic counter-manoeuvres! Once their desired conditions are restored, of course, they will return to their inactivity (until you next disturb them).

It's like a thermostat. If the room is the right temperature, a thermostat doesn't do anything. But if the temperature goes above the required setting, it will turn on the air conditioning straightaway. If you want a higher temperature, it's no use turning on a separate heater, because the thermostat will cancel it out. You need to reset the thermostat itself.

This view makes sense of so much of the endless debates about whether money is a motivator or not. To seek a general answer is to ask the wrong question. Some people are seeking money, others are not. If someone has insufficient funds according to the setting of their 'money-thermostat', the offer of more will appear to motivate them. But once they have enough, they will back off, and providing more money will just make your business poorer.

This is also the mechanism underpinning so much 'resistance' to change. If you want to get someone to go along with your initiative, then if you try to force them, pump them up, energise them or cajole them, you will essentially be trying to disturb them into it. That's where the pushback comes from. Instead, figure out their desired conditions and arrange for them to get what they want by doing what you want.

The best regulation is self-regulation

If you want to ensure that something gets done, the best way is to tap into people's pre-existing motivations. For example:

- In the 1920s, Henry Ford suggested an elegant way to avoid water pollution by proposing that factories could use water as they wanted so long as they put their 'out-pipe upstream from their in-pipe'. You can't motivate people to comply with environmental regulations – I accept that you can force them, but that's different, and invites resistance. However, factory owners are already motivated to ensure they have a clear water supply.
- Yves Morieux gives a great example from the car industry. The manager responsible for ensuring that the car was designed to be easy to repair was informed that once the car went into production he would take charge of the warranty budget.
- The Russian spacecraft Voskhod-1 was so cramped that the cosmonauts could not wear spacesuits. The story goes that one of the engineers warned the chief designer, Sergei Korolev, that the slightest leak of air would kill those on board. Korolev's solution was to appoint the engineer as one of the cosmonauts, figuring that this would help encourage him to make the capsule as safe as possible.

Concluding Thought: Helping Hard-Nosed Managers

I advocate working with the natural dynamics of your organisation, and the natural inclinations of your people, as much as possible. Many leaders find this proposal extremely inspiring – it's great to realise that you can be more effective without having to put in all the energy yourself.

However, some otherwise excellent managers seem to find this kind of approach naïve and touchy-feely. I find they need help in being able to relax their grip. Reminding them of some of this chapters' key examples makes a big difference in helping them to try something new. In particular I point out that:

- the Mars Rover shows how control engineering and information theory *dictate* the need for autonomy at the edge of the organisation;
- the mission command concept was developed in the life-or-death arena of combat – modern military doctrine can't be mistaken for the product of naïveté;
- Sergei Korelev's solution to the overcrowded spacecraft can hardly be thought of as touchy-feely.

Underpinning the idea of giving control to get control is the whole idea that people are 'pre-loaded' with motivation. A practical upshot is a new view of resistance to change and the growth-sapping drag it creates: managers are generally active contributors to resistance. And that means that they can change it.

Chapter 13

Getting Started, Releasing Change

'To know and not to do is to not yet know'

– Harold Milnthorpe

Waiting for Perfect Conditions That Never Come?

My colleague Helga Henry recently sent me an excellent article by Oliver Burkeman.[1] I like Burkeman. While pop psychology is a field full of bunkum (see Box 13.1), he is one of the few writers on the topic worth reading: irreverent, sceptical and sensible.

In the article, Oliver talks about 'The Importance Trap': an often-unrecognised cause of procrastination. He describes The Importance Trap as follows:

Box 13.1
The problem with psychology in management

Psychologists have had a huge influence in business. But caveat emptor! Much of what psychologists have offered is of dubious value outside the laboratory, for at least three reasons.

1 **The replication crisis.** It turns out that much classic psychological research – especially social psychology research that has often been imported into the business world – has been found to be incapable of replication. Even Nobel Laureates have been caught out, so don't think this is just a matter of second-rate practice.

2 **Inappropriate generalisation.** The classic example is the old chestnut about only seven percent of communication being contained in the words people use. Few people seem actually to have read the research, by Albert Meharabian, on which this bit of fake news is based. Meharabian himself is clear that his work has been misunderstood and over-generalised far beyond any useful application, yet trainers trot this stuff out across the globe daily.

3 **The so-called 'Barnum effect'.** Psychological tests and theories often survive because they are *plausible*, and people want them to be true.

These factors mean you have to be very cautious when applying general theories of human behaviour to your specific business. It's why the principles in this book emphasise experimenting with your unique real situation, rather than assuming it will fit some normative framework.

'. . .the way that, the more an activity really matters to you, the more you start to believe you need focus, energy and long stretches of uninterrupted time in which to do it – things that, you tell yourself, you currently lack. And so the less likely you are to do it. *Unimportant stuff gets done; important stuff doesn't.*' [my emphasis].

Oliver gives personal examples, like getting round to reading the Classics. It's vital for business leaders to be very aware of The Importance Trap, too. Because it's a trap that lies in wait not only for individuals, but also for organisations.

I often hear executives talk about some new initiative they need to take. It might be something that would solve a big problem, like getting people to stop over-serving a dwindling market just because it's familiar and comfortable, and instead to focus on a more promising new market. Or it might be something that would create loads of new value, like getting different silos in the business to start working together on innovations that benefit the customer, rather than squabbling over budgets and turf.

Whatever the issue, they'll do a good job of convincing me that it's important and urgent.

Then they'll say: *'But we won't do it YET. I want to WAIT until I can dedicate more resources, give people a good run at it, get these hires completed. . .'*

I call this 'Getting ready to prepare to start to change', and it's one of the major causes of slow progress towards strategic goals.

'But', you might protest, 'I really do need to wait.'

And the rationale will be solid, no doubt.

The thing is, though, that when the appointed time finally comes around, you may find:

- someone else has now grabbed those resources you were going to use;
- the people you earmarked are now busy with other new things (People are *always* too busy, aren't they? They rarely get an absolutely clear run at anything);

- while you've been making those new appointments, one of the existing contributors you were counting on has left your organisation for pastures new.

And perhaps most concerning,

- your competitors have not been waiting for you to get ready.

The timing is never ideal. Sometimes, waiting for it to become ideal is just that: waiting.

One CEO I know has a sign on his wall to inspire him. It shows the words of Marshal Ferdinand Foch, French General and Supreme Allied Commander during the final year of the First World War, credited by historians for the strategy which secured the Allied victory. This is what the sign says:

> Mon centre cède,
> ma droite recule,
> situation excellente,
> j'attaque.

> (My centre is giving way,
> my right is retreating,
> situation excellent,
> I am attacking.)

General Foch understood the danger of the Importance Trap: if you wait for perfect conditions, you will wait a long time (and conditions might actually get much worse). If it's really Important, the time is now.

Exercise
How dangerous is delay?

Think of an important initiative that you are waiting to start because conditions are not yet right. Let's re-examine your assumptions.

1 **Consider ROI**
   - On a scale of 1–10, where 1 is trivial, and 10 is game-changing, how impactful are the potential results of this initiative?
   - What are you losing by delaying? Are you forgoing revenue? Are you disappointing customers? Are you ceding advantage to your competitors?
   - What if you never do this initiative?

2 **Consider the pre-conditions for launching the initiative**
   They are likely to include cash, personnel and time, but there may be others too.
   - Of those pre-conditions that are in place, how sure are you that they will still be available 'when the time is right?' Will you still have the budget? Will you still have key people?
   - Of those pre-conditions that you are waiting for, how many are MUSTS, and how many are just WANTS that you could do without?
   - How many of the pre-conditions you are waiting for could you actually make happen yourself, now, rather than waiting?

3 **Consider consequences**
   - What's the best thing that could happen if you wait?
   - What's the worst thing that could happen if you wait?
   - What's the worst thing that could happen if you get started now?
   - What's the best thing that could happen if you get started now?

	DRIVE	RELEASE
CHANGE	Change-agent pushes, and the system pushes back: resistance	Start with and build on what works
PERFORMANCE	Clear goals and accountabilities with support and feedback	'Somehow' Management

Figure 13.1 Drive performance, but release change

Drive Performance, But Release Change

As we noted in the previous chapter, traditional approaches to change create much of the resistance they defend against. The phrase 'driving change' sounds dynamic, but it's actually a recipe for pushback. Rather than driving change, it's easier and less costly to release it.

The problem of the burning platform

The idea of driving change reaches its zenith with the clichéd image of a 'burning platform'. This is an idea that I find many leaders currently mesmerised by. The image is one of a burning oil rig, and the idea is that if you were unlucky enough to find yourself on one, you would get over any complacency or laziness preventing you from adapting to reality, and would energetically hurl yourself off into the inky black ocean below, trusting somehow that you would be rescued.

I think this might be an OK metaphor in the context of a pre-existing crisis or a turnaround. But that's not what the people I hear seem to mean. They want to *create* a burning platform, and therefore they create urgency.

Why would managers want to create such a situation for their people? And by the way, these same managers then talk about wanting to create employee engagement!

In case you think that I am secretly a softy OD practitioner or whatnot who wants people to link hands and sing Kumbaya, here are three pragmatic and hard-nosed reasons why – outside of genuine crises and turnaround situations – efforts to evoke a burning platform are going to go up in smoke.

- **Denial.** It can actually be pretty hard to convince people that things are as serious as you are trying to make out. The burning platform metaphor ignores the almost infinite human capacity for ignoring or reframing or otherwise rationalising threats – particularly real and genuinely dangerous ones. Cigarette packets have death written all over them, with good reason, yet plenty of people still buy them. Their rationalisation can be subtle. Indeed I know a smoker who only likes to buy packets which warn that 'Cigarettes may harm your unborn child' – because as he is male, he 'reasons' that he will be okay.

- **Lack of direction.** If you scare people, they might move. But they likely won't move in the direction you think they ought to. Instead they scatter. They try desperately to escape. They certainly stop focusing on customers. And you often lose your best people first, since they are the most mobile, and a vicious spiral results.

- **Initiative fatigue.** Even if you can get the result you want with a burning platform approach, you can only do it once, and the cost is high. You can't keep creating crises every six months. And woe betide the manager who keeps starting change initiatives which are abandoned part way through. Such managers are like Matilda in the poem by Hilaire Belloc:

> For every time she shouted 'Fire!',
> They only answered 'Little Liar!'

I have conducted many focus groups with front-line employees and middle managers in my time, and the level of cynicism about grand change initiatives is truly stunning (and often a complete revelation to the senior executives who genuinely think they have achieved 'buy in').

Denial, panic, initiative fatigue – other than that, creating a burning platform is a fine idea.

The dangerous Grand Change Initiative

It's easy to be seduced by the temptation to run a Grand Change Initiative. But such schemes can end badly. It's not just that they often don't work (I will sketch out a few reasons why not below), but it's also that the more bogged-down, half-completed initiatives you start, the more you damage your personal credibility, build cynicism and ultimately risk rendering the organisation unmanageable. Some observations:

- **Most so-called 'resistance' is created by the would-be change agent.** The harder you push, the harder most people will push back. But that's not to say people naturally resist change. You can observe people changing every day. They adapt (often gleefully) to new technology. They accommodate quite quickly to new administrative processes from their banks, local authorities and other institutions – maybe with a bit of grumbling – but they do it most of the time without much fuss. They seek balance and stability, for sure, but they will rebalance quite naturally if presented with the right triggers.

- **Emphasising urgency is counterproductive.** Creating urgency – recommended by some prominent change gurus – sounds good, but actually it's a means masquerading as an end. Of course a rapid tempo is important in business. But my observation is that pursuing urgency directly makes people stick their heads in the sand rather than leading them to face and adapt to an uncomfortable new reality.

- **Kick-off events can be kill-off events.** Big initiatives 'launched' through 'kick-off events', again as recommended by many change experts, are actually great opportunities for the cynics and vested interests to marshal resistance against the change. Sit at the back of one of these events and see for yourself the eye-rolling, conspiratorial nudges and folded arms triggered each time the executive at the front comes out with another dynamic sounding management cliché.

Lip-service buy-in

Everyone knows that early in a change process, you've got to get 'buy in'. Here's the problem though. As we saw in Chapter Seven (Watch what actually happens), people will say they're going to do something, but then they won't follow through. In fact, while I was writing this book, I ran a seminar for a group of CEOs about communicating for change, and when I asked them what was their most common problem, the most popular answer was, 'People pay lip service to changes, then do what they've always done.'

Buy-in has to be more than people saying what they know they're supposed to say.

Release change, then accelerate

To avoid wheel-spin, release change to get things moving, only then step on the gas

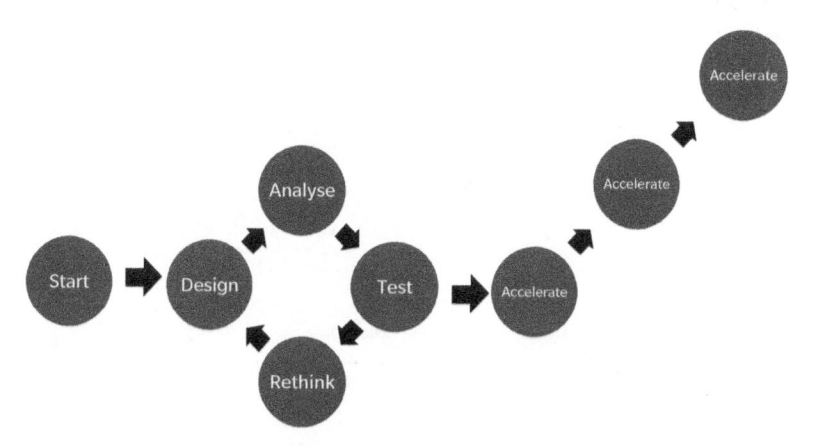

Figure 13.2 Get traction before stepping on the gas

Releasing Change by Starting with What Works

Instead of driving change, let's look to release it. This section offers you a sequence to apply the ideas from the book to create new growth, starting with what works.

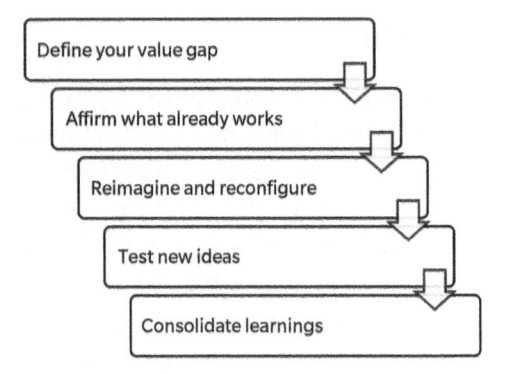

- Define your value gap
- Affirm what already works
- Reimagine and reconfigure
- Test new ideas
- Consolidate learnings

1. Define your value gap

In Chapter 1, we met this chart.

I also gave you a questionnaire to place yourself on the map so you could see where your business is currently located. Depending on your location on that chart, although your goal of Productive Value Creator will be the same, your path will be different.

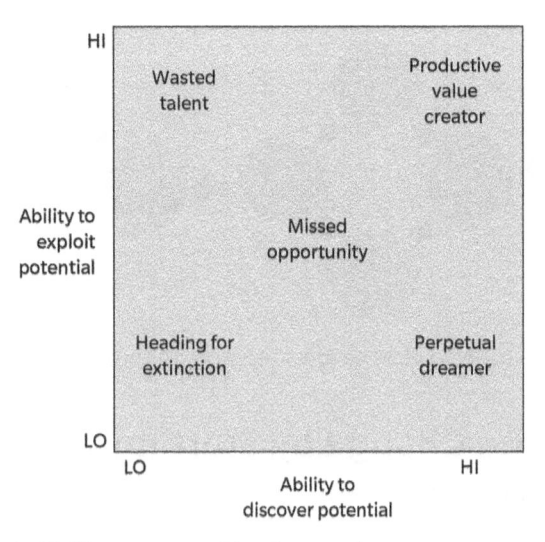

Figure 13.3 Ability to start with what works

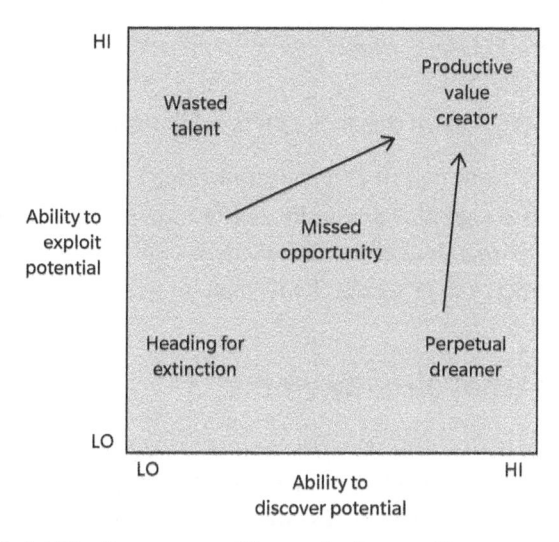

Figure 13.4 What's your specific gap to the goal?

Define your goal in very plain words

The chart is general. Now of course we have to get specific, and to do that, we need to pay attention to Principle Seven: *Use very plain words to describe what you want*. What does Productive Value Creator mean to you? Describe three or four objectives in very plain words. You can apply the Troubleshooter TV Documentary technique (see Chapter 9) to help: imagine that a film crew made a documentary about the desired transition. What would we see and hear by the final episode that would demonstrate success?

Assess the value of closing the gap

You need to get a good ROI to justify the effort of closing the gap! In order to assess the potential, here are some questions to answer:

- How will we assess the value of achieving the goal?
- What is the impact on sales, costs, profit, cash, revenue, return on capital?
- What new opportunities will be opened up by achieving this?

Start with what works

- What's the intangible impact on our brand, our reputation with talent, our appeal to investors?
- What difference will this make to my leadership and its legacy?

Be ambitious in your goals and conservative in your estimates. This will help you decide how much time, effort and expense to put in. Don't try and use a sledgehammer to crack a nut, but don't use a pea-shooter to try to bring down an elephant.

2. Affirm what already works

Once you are really clear on what exactly being a productive value creator looks like, you can use the scaling technique we met in Chapter 5 to zero in on *what already works*. This is going to be where we start to dig for the hidden gold. So start by identifying where you are now on a scale from 1 to 10. Let's call that LEVEL N.

Don't be too concerned if you score yourself rather low. Remember the shopping centre director we met in Chapter 5? He was demoralised because of a disappointing employee survey, but once

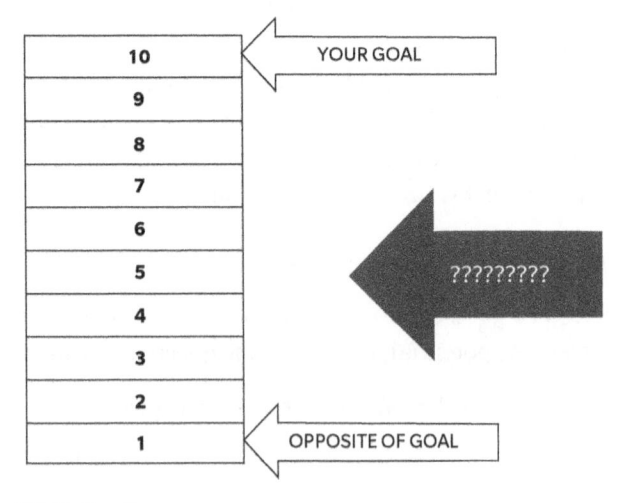

Figure 13.5 Scaling

we started to look at what was going right, he saw that he could address the employee issue, and build a better future for the organisation, from a much stronger foundation than he thought.

So, once you've assessed your position, ask yourself, 'How come we aren't worse? Why aren't we on LEVEL N-1?' (i.e. If you gave yourself 5/10, for example, how come you aren't a 4?). List out as many reasons as you can for why you didn't score yourself lower: this will give you a list of what works. You can apply techniques from Chapters 4 and 5 to mine this list for hidden gold.

3. Reimagine and reconfigure your resources

Start to wonder what it could be like one rung higher on the scale, at LEVEL N+1. What new value might you be bringing to the market? We've looked at many tools you can use to help. One of the best is the Car Wash framework we met in Chapter 3. This is also a great time to bring customers inside to get their ideas (Chapter 11).

4. Test your new ideas

As you get new ideas, ask, 'What would have to happen for this next step up to come about? What would have to be true? How can we test these hypotheses by letting the world teach us what works?' (Chapter 6).

5. Consolidate and share learnings

Repeat the activities of steps 2, 3 and 4 until you are confident that you have ideas with traction. Share your initial successes around the organisation, for example with Show and Tell sessions. It's far more credible for your own people to tell warts-and-all stories about their experiments than it is to have kick-off meetings full of slick PowerPoint and unsubstantiated promise.

Accelerating change

Getting the ball rolling is a real achievement. But it's too soon to declare victory. Getting to LEVEL N+1 is not the same as getting to your ideal Productive Value Creator position. Now that you've got demonstrated traction, it's time to step on the gas and accelerate.

> **Box 13.2**
> **Alchemical acceleration**
>
> In Chapter 3, we borrowed a metaphor from alchemy when we looked at ways to recombine existing assets to create new and greater value. The alchemists had another fascinating notion that can help us think about accelerating change. They hypothesised that, under the correct circumstances, all manifestations of matter evolve naturally from basic elements. They thought that while usually this process is undetectably slow, it could happen more quickly in principle, and indeed reasoned that this must have been the case at the dawn of creation. Their idea was that nature is often busy doing next to nothing, and they were attracted by the possibilities of giving it the 'hurry up'.[2] That's appealing in business, as well. After all, who hasn't felt at one time or another that their organisation is busy doing next to nothing?

For whatever reasons, result-producing processes tend to proceed more slowly than they need to. I've found that most experienced business people readily accept that hypothesis.

And what are the main reasons? At the risk of an over-generalisation, here is my observation. Some people are busy setting inspiring visions and stretch goals for others, but without adequate attention to the means whereby these aspirations will be achieved – in other words, they're attempting to practice the *Somehow Management* we met in Chapter 10. Others are busily absorbed on the highways – and more often by-ways – of methodology and process, and lose sight of the goal. They go round the houses to get next door. They create what I like to call 'epiphenomenal work'.

Banish 'epiphenomenal work'

An epiphenomenon is something that accompanies a phenomenon you are interested in, but doesn't contribute to its purpose. For example, noise is an epiphenomenon of a lawn-mower, and it actually represents work (moving around a lot of air molecules) that makes no contribution to cutting grass. By *epiphenomenal work* I mean effort that goes on in organisations without actually contributing anything.

As Nietzsche pointed out (Chapter 8), there's an all-too-human tendency to get more interested in means than ends. We might go for a walk on a Sunday with no particular destination in mind, and meander around the far side of the lake, finally ending up at a café after a leisurely stroll. The journey provides its own justification. But on Monday – when we need a quick sandwich for lunch – it's quicker to call and get it delivered.

Accelerative thinking

Not surprisingly, the biggest drag on our acceleration has to do with the way we think about time. We tend to expect the future to proceed incrementally from the present, and assume that the way things will happen will pretty much be the way things have happened in the past. These assumptions underlie most of the business planning I see. Here are some of the main problems:

- Plans based on extrapolations from the past tend to keep you going in the same general direction. They don't address the issue of whether that's where you want to go, or need to go, next.
- Plans based on extrapolation tend to assume that external conditions will remain more or less the same – clearly a dangerous basis on which to proceed. What if the market is drying up? What if new competitors or technological trends are going to make your products obsolete? Norton doesn't sell many motorbikes any more.

Start with what works

- The level at which longer-term goals are set is determined by current and past limitations. This is one of the problems with the popular idea of SMART goals. The R stands for realistic. Realistic according to what standards? The answer is always going to be in according to the standards of past experience – fine for performance management perhaps, but destined only to be a drag on any serious effort at innovation.
- When you plan by extrapolation, you make assumptions about how long things need to take, based on how long they have taken in the past.

Reasoning forwards like this means that exciting futures which are perfectly possible can *seem* destined to stay forever over the horizon.

Elon Musk, CEO of Tesla Motors and Space X, has spoken about the difference of thinking by analogy vs thinking from first principles. Space X entered a market where people thought about new rocket designs by analogy with existing designs (what I describe as thinking from the past to the present to the future). As a result of this thinking process, space launch vehicle prices had been flat-to-slightly-increasing for years. But Musk and his colleagues noted that the price of the bill of materials for a rocket was a small fraction of the cost of then-current rockets. Therefore, he concluded, there was the opportunity for a fundamental rethink to dramatically improve results. He and his colleagues rethought rocket launchers from first principles and created a launcher for a few percent of the going rate. Another engineer John Boyd – the former dogfighting instructor and strategist we met in Chapter 8 – did something very similar with the engine of the F-16.

That's great for engineers dealing with physics-based problems. But the idea applies far more widely. How can you escape from the limitations on your business that are imposed by thinking by analogy from past, to present, to future?

By reversing from the desired future into the present, it's possible to avoid falling foul of past, learned limitations. It has to be said that starting with the future requires considerable mental agility in practice, and many managers who recognise the value of the idea don't do it simply because they just don't have the tools.

Below is a process that I've used successfully with leaders, teams, and individual contributors on many occasions. It allows you to suspend assumptions about what's possible long enough to develop actionable plans for achieving big goals. It uses the idea of a timeline – either physically laid out on the floor, or on a table top, flip-chart or whiteboard as appropriate. I'll explain it as if you are going to walk through it on the floor because many clients find this approach works best.

The technique I describe helps you disengage from assumed limitations fast. It works phenomenally well for individuals and organisations alike. I've used it to help an unknown provincial art lecturer become a sought-after painter selling canvases for five figures at one-man shows in London and New York, a divisional vice-president mobilise a new country-wide growth push worth $100 million and a former Mars executive develop a revolutionary social impact investment vehicle to transform the fortunes of a coastal town that had fallen on challenging times.

Exercise
Back from the future

Identify and stand on a timeline, starting from the present and looking out into the future.

(Present) ···························· ▶ Future
Timeline

Pick a really big, worthwhile, motivating goal, without, at this stage, being concerned about how realistic it is.

(Present)   (Goal)

223

Step off the timeline and stand in a position as an observer. Imagine 'someone' is successfully involved in achieving that unreasonable goal.

(Stand)

(Present) ('Someone')

Then identify the step just before 'that someone' achieved the goal. Ask the key question:

> 'What has to already be there (or be true) in order for "that someone" to achieve the goal as a natural next step?'

Step into that position and check that if you were there, you could take the next step and realise the goal.

(Present)   (?) ---> Natural Next Step (Goal)

The position you've identified now becomes the new (stepping stone) goal.

(Present)   (Stepping) ---> (Goal)

Now ask yourself:

> 'Is the stepping stone an unreasonable goal for me – or could I just get it done with what I have already?'

If it is still out of reach, use the same process again, this time making the stepping stone the goal for 'someone' (as in step 3) and identify the step before it (using the key questions from step 4). Keep going until you reach a 'reasonable' stepping stone you can just make happen from your present platform.

If the stepping stone is reasonable – you're ready to go.

Present → Stepping → Stepping → Stepping → Goal

The trick to this technique is in how rigorous you are when you ask the question 'What has to *already* be there (or be true) in order for "that someone" to achieve the goal as a natural next step?' i.e. not what would have to be true for you.

'That someone' is not subject to the same imagined limits that you are imposing on yourself.

> ### Box 13.3
> #### Who captures the value?
>
> A key premise of the 'start with what works' approach is that people are too quick to look outside for 'saviours'. Starting with what works is far more likely to lead you to distinctive advantages. It has another strategic benefit too. One of the biggest questions in business strategy is: 'Who captures the value?' If you are prepared to do the work of not needing a saviour, you can capture value from customers who are not willing to do that thinking – you become *their* saviour.

Things to Remember

There are lots of ways to apply the principles in this book. In this chapter we've looked at one way to string them together. You will inevitably have to adapt this scheme to your personal circumstances, but these steps will be a good starting point.

Before we summarise the Do's, let's recall a couple of important Don'ts:

- Don't wait for ideal conditions that will never come.
- Don't drive change; seek to release it.

Here are the steps again:

1 Define your value gap. Clarify what you want in plain words, and get a clear sense of the ROI for making the change.
2 Affirm what already works. Use the techniques we've met throughout the book to track down your hidden and underappreciated resources.
3 Reimagine and reconfigure your resources in line with emerging customer needs.
4 Consolidate learnings. Let the world teach you what works, and keep tweaking your approach until you have a confident platform for change.
5 Accelerate change. Once you are sure of your assumptions, you can work backwards to figure out the fastest way to achieve the growth you seek.

The important thing, as we said at the start of the chapter, is to actually do it: to use these alchemical keys to unlock your hidden gold.

In the epilogue, we'll take a look at applying the same ideas to yourself as a leader.

Chapter 14

Epilogue: You Go First

If you've ever studied martial arts, or watched films like *The Karate Kid*, you no doubt know the Japanese term *Sensei*. Even if it's never been properly translated for you, you probably assume that Sensei simply means teacher. And of course it does mean that. But it also means 'one who has gone before.'

The best way to understand how to start with what works is to engage in it personally. So here in the Epilogue I invite you – whether you're already an established leader or whether you're currently an ambitious individual contributor – to go through the processes we've looked at yourself. Because having 'gone before' your organisation, you will be that much better equipped to act as the Sensei.

And there's another related sense of this idea of 'going before'. It has to do with vision. The leaders we call visionary 'go before' the organisations they lead. Their thinking is way out in front. The organisation is not simply an end in itself, and it's not just a vehicle for their personal enrichment. They are trying to achieve something bigger through their organisation. In a way, the organisation becomes a vehicle for their values.

It's easy enough to see this in the case of a Steve Jobs, or an Elon Musk, or an Anita Roddick. These people had something they cared about beyond Apple, Tesla or Body Shop. They built their organisations to create legs under their visions (contrast that to the professional corporate plutocrats motivated solely by stock options and status).

Of course, most business people – whatever the size of their organisation – are neither celebrity entrepreneurs nor shadowy plutocrats. But they all have to manage the tension between the important but mundane job of hitting their numbers, and the rewards of building a meaningful career and personal legacy.

The Demands of the Day Job

Many leaders have heard the following excuse for not innovating or changing: 'I would have, but I had to look after the day job.' Yet if they are honest, the leaders struggle with the same issue. What are the things that take up a leader's time and keep them from fulfilling their potential? The list is long, but some of the ones I hear most from my clients are:

- getting pulled into operational minutiae;
- a queue of people wanting you to solve their problems;
- being called upon to adjudicate on disputes that should have been sorted out at lower levels;
- computerised interruptions such as unnecessary meeting requests and email 'cc's.

Leaders know they and their organisations have to be more strategic, but they often abdicate a better future because of current demands. They fall foul of an unconscious conspiracy to slow their success (see Box 14.1).

Box 14.1
The unconscious conspiracy against the leader

Warren Bennis was a hugely influential authority on leadership, a Pulitzer Prize nominated writer, and had significant leadership experience both as an infantry officer in WWII and later as the President of the University of Cincinnati. His most striking book title is *The Unconscious Conspiracy: Why Leaders Can't Lead*. In it, he describes his efforts to figure out why his organisation wasn't making progress on its strategic goals. He describes his shock when, after inspecting his clogged calendar, he suddenly awoke to 'a vast, amorphous, unwitting, unconscious conspiracy to prevent me from doing anything whatever to change the . . . status quo'. He identified two challenges relevant to anyone trying to get things done in an organisation: not only how to deal with 'the turmoil and inertia that threaten the best-laid plans,' but also 'how to keep *routine* from sapping their ability to make a real impact'. [my emphasis].

Getting out ahead of your organisation

It's a commonplace thing to say that leaders need personal agility in a world where technological disruption, climate change, demographic shifts and a global pandemic keep upending things. It's commonplace, but that doesn't make it easier.

We human beings have – *at the biological level* – a predilection towards habit. In particular, people are reluctant to give up things that have worked in the past. That's one reason why starting with what works is a good idea. We aren't asked to abandon what's worked; we instead work to *utilise* it for new purposes.

Anyway, the fact is, if you expect your organisation to change, you will have to go first.

The only way to change behaviour

There is only one way to change someone else's behaviour. It's the same whether it's a direct report, a customer, a boss, an audience or a team.

How do you do it? You need to change *your* behaviour in relation to their behaviour. This is both bad news and good news. The bad news is that what you are doing or saying may be the very thing keeping a problem in place. The good news is you therefore have the power to change it.

This first became clear to me after a fascinating afternoon many years ago talking to a top dog trainer. After she had shown me around the kennels, the trainer let me in on a secret: dog training is not for the dog. It's for the owner.

Dogs are uncooperative because of the cues they get from their humans.

For example, the trainer explained:

'If the dog stands in front of the TV, most people shout: "Get out of the way, Alfie!"'

'But Alfie doesn't understand this the way the owner intends. To Alfie, this shouting is not a warning to move. It's actually welcome attention. From it, Alfie learns that if he wants more attention, all he has to do is stand in front of the TV.'

'What the owner should do is wait for Alfie to sit somewhere away from the TV screen, and then make a fuss of rewarding him. Now when Alfie wants attention he can go to that spot.'

'I teach dog owners to amplify helpful behaviours and not give oxygen to unhelpful ones. That way, the helpful stuff starts to crowd out the unhelpful.'

'And it works with people, too,' she confided.

(Just as she said this, I noticed her husband putting a cup of tea on the table beside me. He looked over to his wife, who nodded approvingly, and then he trotted happily back into the kitchen. And then she winked at me.)

Joking apart, there's a very important lesson here. Amplifying helpful responses, and simply withholding reinforcement from unhelpful ones, is an effective way to shape unfolding circumstances. In other words: if you want to change behaviour, start with what works!

Apparently, most dog owners are not naturals at this: they tend to focus on what isn't working, be it the dog pulling on their lead or barking at passers-by. The trainer made it clear that if you can change the owners, the dogs change too. The same goes for leadership. Change yourself and change your world.

What kind of leader do you want to be?

One of the best coaching questions to ask leaders looking to make a big leap forward is, 'What *kind* of leader do you want to be?' There's something about this question that connects people up to a bigger frame of reference. That is often enough to help them see their way clear.

Here's a framework from the work of Robert Dilts[1] that is very effective in thinking about the kind of person you need to be to achieve *your* leap.

Let's walk through it. Open up a laptop so you can take notes and fill in your own ideas.

Level	Prompt (ABCDE)	Description
A. Identity	I Am . . .	
B. Beliefs & Values	I Believe . . . I Value . . .	
C. Capabilities & Skills	I Can . . .	
D. Behaviours	I Do . . .	
E. Environment	Where, when, with whom . . .	

Figure 14.1 Dilts' logical levels

The idea is that each level in the framework governs the next lower level. Ideally, all the levels need to line up and support one another. Although when we apply it to your situation, we'll start from the top, it's easier to understand how it works starting at the bottom.

Here's how I usually explain it to audiences: 'Let's say you go to a relaxed party. That's the ENVIRONMENT (bottom level of the framework). In that environment, would you say that you could meet someone for the first time, and without any planning, spend 5–10 minutes telling them about your job, your industry, the factors affecting the sector and so on?'

It's very likely. Whenever I've asked audiences, they vigorously nod their head, 'Yes.' They'd easily come up with that BEHAVIOUR (next level up) in that environment. They have the CAPABILITY, after all, and they'd use it. No problem.

Then I ask my audiences a new question: 'If, instead of this happening at a party, I asked you to go to a thousand-seat auditorium, with tiered seating, stage lights and two TV cameras, how many of you could still talk extemporaneously about your work?'

Many people now shake their heads 'No'.

This is interesting. They must still have the CAPABILITY, the skill, but in the new environment, they don't produce the behaviour. What's going on?

Well the idea is that the ability to deploy the capability, to manifest it into behaviour, is controlled by the next higher level: their BELIEFS. If you believe a big presentation is a chance to be humiliated in front of a group of strangers, then you'll not access your capability. You won't express it as behaviour. On the other hand, if you believe, as I do after years of experience, that presenting to big audiences is huge fun, then I think you'll agree that's going to give you much better access to your capabilities.

Oh by the way, it wasn't always that way for me. I started my career as a University lecturer. I was pretty hopeless to start with.

Students used to come to the beginning of the lecture, take a handout, and then leave before I started to speak!

Other lecturers struggled too. In fact I had one colleague who needed a whisky before he lectured, just to get through the damn thing. As I thought at that time that lecturing was going to be my career, I decided I better do something healthier. So I started to take classes and over time I developed competence and supporting beliefs, and as I was rewarded with success, I developed the IDENTITY of a PRESENTER. I took more courses, tried out ideas and did more of whatever worked. The next level was to think of myself as a SPEAKER, which was even more empowering. Once I started getting paid, and got an agent, I started to think of myself as a PROFESSIONAL SPEAKER. I can tell you that once you really see yourself as a Professional Speaker, all the levels line up very nicely.

How do you need to see yourself to be the leader you want to be? A couple of powerful generic identity statements for executives are Visionary and Dealmaker. Two good ones for professionals are Rainmaker and Trusted Advisor. Any of these are well worth pursuing if they resonate with you, but also try and come up with something with unique significance for you – you don't have to tell anyone else what it is.

Once you've got the desired IDENTITY statement, the next thing is to fill out the other levels of framework. Don't think you have to approach them in order. If one area strikes you as of particular interest, dive in and develop it. For a visionary leader it might start out like this:

What does your next level look like to you? (Note: the more detail you can come up with, the better. Push yourself. Ask 'What else? What else?' Get a trusted advisor to help).

Once you've got a sense of the leader you want to be for your next leap, you can utilise the methods we've looked at throughout the book to look inside for your own hidden gold and make the personal transformation. Let's look at that process at a high level so you can get the big picture.

Level	Prompt (ABCDE)	Description
A. Identity	I Am . . .	a Visionary leader, a Value-creator
B. Beliefs & Values	I Believe . . .	I'm able to bring resources together to create new value etc
	I Value . . .	Sustainable growth etc
C. Capabilities and Skills	I Can . . .	Formulate compelling value propositions Pitch persuasively Negotiate Raise capital etc
D. Behaviours	I Do . . .	Create high-growth businesses
E. Environment	Where, when, with whom . . .	Market analysts and investors on investor relations calls Board members in corporate boardrooms C-level executives at potential customers and suppliers

Figure 14.2 Logical levels example for a 'visionary leader'

Finding your personal hidden resources

We've met a number of techniques that can be applied to the search for individual resources. In particular, you should consider using *Scaling* (Chapter 5 and Chapter 13) augmented by the *Total Person Inventory* (Chapter 10).

Scaling

By now this pattern of questioning should be familiar. Ask yourself, 'On a scale from 1 to 10, where 10 represents the leader I want to be, where am I now?' Let's say you give yourself a 6.

The next question is: 'How come I'm not just a 5?' In answering, you want to take the time, and put in the effort, to generate an exhaustive list.

To go even further, you can fill out a Total Person Inventory for yourself (see Chapter 10). For example, Figure 14.3 shows one that one of my clients came up with.

Accomplishments in Previous Jobs, Hobbies, Interests	So: Capabilities...	Which implies other resources...
Delivered risk management system for ABC bank	• Project management/ execution • Sustaining motivation of a team • Dealing with difficult stakeholders • Dealing with regulators	• Coaching • Briefing meetings • Expectations management • Negotiation • Educating non-technical 'buyers'
Treasurer of a local charity – applied for a grant to better serve beneficiaries	• Grant-writing • Making a compelling case • Understanding funding landscape • Understanding factors influencing funders • Demonstrating ROI	• Influencing skills • Political and economic awareness • Self-motivation to contribute to causes beyond own interests
Biochemistry graduate – has maintained interest even though now working outside the field	• Ability to assimilate scientific research publications • Predisposition to evidence-based reasoning	• Ability to engage with technical experts • Ability to sort wheat from chaff when dealing with technologists

Figure 14.3 Total person inventory example

Again, having a trusted advisor to help with this is invaluable. You are so familiar with yourself that you could miss the really good stuff. Getting other people to contribute their perspective makes a lot of sense. When I've conducted 360-degree interviews for clients, we've often uncovered hidden personal resources this way.

> **Box 14.2**
> **Transmuting the negative**
>
> Even unhelpful response patterns can sometimes be repurposed if you recognise their positive qualities. For example, sarcastic people often demonstrate great wit and mental agility. Cynics are often the first to see fatal flaws in arguments – annoying but potentially invaluable. And Andy Grove, co-founder of Intel wrote a classic book on innovation entitled *Only the Paranoid Survive*.

So, you've explored why you are not one level lower on your scale and completed a *Total Person Inventory*. These two techniques make you focus on what already works. They typically connect people with a great sense of resourcefulness. You can now use this resourcefulness to take a decisive step towards being the leader you envisioned earlier.

Ask yourself what it would be like if you were operating at one level up the scale from where you initially placed yourself. What would you be doing? Where? With whom? How would that be different and better? Then ask yourself:

> 'Given the platform of resources I've identified, what can I do to make that next level a reality?'

You will probably find that you can make more progress, more easily than you earlier thought possible.

Still waiting for better conditions before you start?

Let's say you're keen to start with what works, but you just can't make the space to get started. Maybe you suspect you are suffering at the hand of an unconscious conspiracy to slow you down! Or maybe things are going really well – you're nearly there – but you meet a sting in the tail – the feeling of resistance that often accompanies efforts to get things over the line. What can you do? A practical response is to make three lists.

1. First, a TO STOP list in order to release resources (time, energy, people, money etc.) for more productive uses. Most organisations and individuals are doing things that, while important at one time, now no longer make sense, or are better done by someone else. The question to ask is: 'If we weren't doing this already, would we start doing it today?' If not, then put it on the TO STOP list, and act accordingly.

2. A SNAGS list. Over time, we – both as individuals and organisations – accumulate workarounds. These are temporary or less-than-ideal 'solutions', which become habits. In time, our repertoire or standard ways of operating are dominated by them. For example:

    - Someone is promoted to babysit a dysfunctional team, and then starts to acquire an empire while the fundamentals are never sorted out.

    - A hand-updated, error-prone spreadsheet is controlled by one bottleneck person, where instead there should be a widely accessible database (for which you probably already have the licences).

    - Space is used for temporary storage but becomes de facto warehousing, while staff are crammed into an unsuitably small office area.

    Making a SNAGS list and picking off a few easy ones straightaway liberates a lot of energy.

3. Drawing on what you've learned from the first two lists, you can finally turn your attention to a TO DO list. We all have TO DO lists, but do we honestly work through them in the best order? Try prioritising tasks from most productive to least productive, then do the most productive first. Unfortunately, that often means 'most uncomfortable first'. That might mean calling a customer before scheduling an internal progress meeting or addressing a conflict in the team before a general catch-up on industry news. Doing lower priority tasks first is often a kind of procrastination – you can see you've ticked a lot of items off at the end of the day, but if they aren't the big, often more uncomfortable, ones you could be busy doing nothing. Most people find that having someone to keep them accountable is a big help.

These suggestions are extremely simple – so simple that it would be easy to overlook their power and to say 'Oh, yes. Already know that'. However, as a mentor of mine used to say: 'To know and not do is to not yet know.' The Three Lists exercise is a very fast way to create space to do new things.

How Fast Will You Grow?

Sometimes when I talk to clients, they wonder if starting with what works is going to be a quick fix. And sometimes that does happen. For others though, it might take a while to find the right combination of resources – one that will create a real sustainable breakthrough. That's true for both companies and individuals. For example:

- **Arianna Huffington** founded *The Huffington Post* at age 55. Huffington had a varied early career, among other things working as a political commentator and writer. Those experiences helped her develop a wide base of resources. But it was only when she combined those resources into a new configuration – one that met the emerging needs of media consumers in a unique way – that she became a household name. HuffPost later sold to AOL for $315 million.

Epilogue: You Go First

- **Vera Wang.** Wang is world-famous for designing iconic gowns but she didn't start out in fashion. In fact she was originally a figure skater, but failed to reach the top rank. She then studied journalism. That led to a job at Vogue, where she quickly rose to become their senior fashion editor. She held that role for 15 years then spent a spell at Ralph Lauren. When she got married, she was disappointed by the wedding dresses on offer, so she decided to design her own. One year later she opened her first bridal boutique in New York. As well as her huge success as a dress designer, she has designed many outfits for the US Olympic Skating Team and in 2009 was inducted into the Figure Skating Hall of Fame.

- **Reid Hoffman.** After studying cognitive science and philosophy, Hoffman intended to become a professor and public intellectual. He decided however that he would have more impact in the world as an entrepreneur. He worked for a winery, then for Apple, where he attempted to set up an early form of social networking. After a spell at Fujistu, in 1997 he formed another early social networking platform called SocialNet. He then became COO at PayPal where he was described as 'firefighter-in-chief'. He got an incredibly wide range of experience at PayPal: he was responsible for all external relationships, including with payments providers, commercial partners, government and professional advisors. When PayPal was acquired by eBay, Hoffman applied all he had learned to launch LinkedIn.

- **Stefani Germanotta, also known as Lady Gaga.** Clearly Lady Gaga has talents as a singer, songwriter and performer. Yet while these are world class, they are arguably not enough in themselves to have given her such breakthrough results. Neither, on its own, is her capacity for being outrageous. So what was her hidden gold? Here are a couple of examples. When she was at school, she was the weird kid. For many people that wouldn't have been an asset, but she reframed it and used it to build a unique relationship with her fan base, calling them her 'Little Monsters', and reassuring them about the value of their idiosyncrasies. Another valuable but less apparent resource is her ability to bring talented people together to help her. She used these skills to build up a group of people that became known as the Haus of Gaga. This group of artists and designers travel with her on tour and help her develop and execute her creative vision. Subsequently she's been able to build further on these resources. In 2019, Lady Gaga joined up with Amazon to launch a gender-neutral makeup line, 'Haus Laboratories' – again recombining her brand, creative team and relationship-building skills to create further leverage.

Each of these examples enjoyed some early successes. But they only displayed their full potential once they found their winning combination of resources. And – importantly – all of them have enjoyed continuing growth by reconfiguring those resources to meet new challenges and opportunities.

The great advantage of starting with what works is that by basing your next moves on successes and strengths, you and your business can continue to grow in a fast-changing world, and you'll do so with less risk and in a way only you can.

Further Resources

Go to *bassclusker.com/swww* – for further help in applying the *start with what works* approach in your organisation.

Notes

Chapter 1

1. 'Moonshot' projects are inspiring, no doubt, but they're often shots in the dark. And if you consider the original moonshot – the dramatically successful Apollo space programme – it created fewer valuable applications than the cheaper and far easier-to-build orbital launchers that give us services like GPS.

Chapter 2

1. Dryburgh, Alastair (2011) *Everything You Know About Business Is Wrong: How to unstick your thinking and upgrade your rules of thumb.* Headline.

Chapter 3

1. VUCA is an acronym for Volatile, Uncertain, Complex and Ambiguous. The term originated in military circles but has become popular in the business world.
2. The *Chymistry of Isaac Newton Project*, based at the University of Indiana, and a collaborator with *The Newton Project* at the University of Oxford, is devoted to the editing and exposition of Newton's alchemical work.

Notes

3. Professor Tim Baines at Aston Business School goes further and suggests rethinking your products as a service that your customer uses up over time.

4. This may be to do with prevailing tastes or more likely because in many Asian cultures, jewellery has often been used as a store of personal wealth, in preference to an historically under-developed banking system.

5. Sutherland, Rory (2019) *Alchemy: The Surprising Power of Ideas That Don't Make Sense*. Virgin Digital.

6. Schwartz, Barry (2009) *The Paradox of Choice: Why More Is Less*. HarperCollin.

Chapter 4

1. Dr James Wilk drew my attention to Bacon's distinction between the realms in which our ideas either 1) bear fruit or 2) bring light. It's invaluable to be able to shift back and forth between considering our reasons for being interested in a technology versus thinking about how that technology works in itself.

2. For example, Jay Barney (*Gaining and Sustaining Competitive Advantage*, Addison-Wesley (1996)) and Michael Porter (For a very clear and authoritative introduction to Porter's work, see *Understanding Michael Porter* by Jean Magretta, Harvard Business Review Press (2011)).

3. The categorisation is my modification and extension of the work of Slywotsky et al. (2003). (Slywotzky, Adrian J., Wise, Richard and Weber, Karl (2003) *How to Grow When Markets Don't*. Warner Books.)

Chapter 5

1. Boyd, Drew and Goldenberg, Jacob (2013) *Inside The Box: A proven system of creativity for breakthrough results*. Simon & Schuster.

2. Koch, Robert (2011) *The 80/20 Principle: The secret of achieving more with less*. Nicholas Brealey Publishing.

3. Nassim Nicholas Taleb (2013) *Antifragile: Things that gain from disorder*. Penguin.

Chapter 6

1. Goldman, William (1996) *Adventures in The Screen Trade: A personal view of Hollywood*. Abacus.

2. Enron was an energy trading company named by *Fortune* magazine as 'America's Most Innovative Company' for six consecutive years. It collapsed after the discovery of a massive accounting fraud. Its 2001 bankruptcy filing was the largest in American history at the time with losses totalling around $74 billion.

3. Mintzberg, Henry (2001) How to overcome change fatigue. *Harvard Management Communication Letter*, Vol. 4, No. 7, July 2001.

4. Sources for these: Osterwalder & Pigneur (2010) *Business Model Generation* Wiley; Ash Maurya (2012) *Running Lean*, O'Reilly; Kaplan & Norton (2004); *Strategy Maps*; Tregoe and Zimmerman (1980) *Top Management Strategy*, Simon & Schuster.

5. This was pre-COVID-19. Since then, we've learned that we can do a lot of things remotely that we thought were impossible, or at least of unacceptable quality. Indeed, the COVID-19 crisis has provided many dramatic demonstrations of our ability to do more than we thought we could with what we already had.

Chapter 7

1. Some people worry that this is deceptive. I'd argue that a leader's greater responsibility is to promote the success of the company, and that's what will most benefit employees as well as customers and owners. The point is not to play 'Gotcha' – I'm certainly against that. But it's an abdication of responsibility not to make sure you are aware of what really happens on 'on the ground'.

Notes

2. One of the pioneers of cybernetics, the trans-disciplinary study of effective organisation, control, regulation and communication.

Chapter 8

1. This is a classic example of *Frugal Innovation*. See Radjou, Navi and Prabhu, Jaideep (2015) *Frugal Innovation: How to do better with less*. Economist Books.

2. Coram, Robert (2004) *Boyd: The Fighter Pilot Who Changed the Art of War*. Back Bay Book.

Chapter 9

1. I learned about denominalising abstract nouns from Grinder and Bandler (Bandler, Richard and Grinder, John (1975) *The Structure of Magic: A Book about Language and Therapy*, Volume 1. Science and Behavior Books). They present their analysis of questions asked by outstanding psychotherapists.

Chapter 10

1. This disguised example is based on a real company operating in the 1950s and 60s. While technology changes, human nature doesn't. The example is eerily evocative of stories that came out of Boeing in the wake of the 737 Max accidents of 2018/19.

2. I originally learned the cross-pollination technique from Alan Weiss.

3. Open Space was originated by Harrison Owen, and it's in the public domain. It's worth reading Owen's work if you want to get more information before trying it. While it can easily be run internally by someone who has been through the process once or twice, it's worth hiring an experienced facilitator for the first time you do it.

Chapter 11

1. COVID-19 has had a dramatic effect on the use of physical space by businesses. How usage will change from here is unclear. What *is* clear is that leaders should be thinking about how shifts online and changes in physical space usage affect relationships with customers (not to mention suppliers, partners and other stakeholders).

2. Donald Miller's book *Storybrand* (Miller, Donald (2017) *Building a Storybrand: Clarify your message so customers will listen*. HarperCollins Leadership) clearly lays out this idea from a brand positioning point of view.

3. All this may actually have become easier since the COVD-19 crisis. Boundaries between customers, employees and senior leaders need not be as solid as they once were with everyone so clearly just a video call away.

Chapter 12

1. For more on responsabilisation, see Harnessing Everyday Genius by Gary Hamel and Michele Zanini, *Harvard Business Review* July–August 2020 Issue. And *Explainer: Michelin's 'responsabilisation'*, FT.com

2. This idea was pioneered by Robert Schaffer who discussed it in a number of books and articles including *High Impact Consulting* (Schaffer, Robert H. (2002) *High-impact Consulting: How clients and consultants can leverage rapid results into long-term gains*, Wiley.).

Chapter 13

1. *Guardian* 19 May 2017.

2. While alchemists' ideas about the mechanisms involved aren't borne out by modern science, it turns that there certainly are

natural processes that can be accelerated to their end point under the right circumstances – in fact that's exactly the purpose of a catalyst.

Chapter 14

1. Dilts, Robert (2017) *Visionary Leadership Skills: Creating a world to which people want to belong.* Dilts Strategy Group.

Index

accelerative thinking 221–3
access point 64
acquisition 23
agility 89–90, 153
alchemy 12, 35
Alchemy: The Surprising Power of Ideas That Don't Make Sense (Sutherland) 49, 110
Alphabet 154
Alstom 43
alumni networks 63
Amazon 95
Amazon Web Services (AWS) 3, 54
Anand, Rooney 83
Ann Summers 110
Antifragile (Taleb) 90
antifragility 90
Apple 5, 44, 56, 57, 70
Aquafaba 87
ARM 61

Arm and Hammer's products 54
artificial intelligence (AI) 24, 146–50
Arup 61
assumptions
  critical/leap of faith 101–3
  identifying and testing 94, 98, 103–5
  ranking 103, 104
Augmented Reality 114
AW&B 162–3

Bacon, Francis 53, 93
Baines, Tim 244
baking soda, purpose of 53–4
Ballmer, Steve 97, 98
Barney, Jay 56, 57
Barnum effect 208
base *vs* alchemical value 38–9
Basecamp 65, 69
bassclusker.com 241

Index

behaviour
   as best information 110
   change 230–1
Belloc, Hilaire 213
Bennis, Warren 229
Benoit 156
Big Four Accountancy
   practices 68
Bostrom, Nick 26
Boyd, Drew 85
Boyd, John R. 136–7, 197, 222
Boyle, Robert 35
buffering 89
bundles
   framework for developing 44–7
   refining 48–51
   using to transmuting business 40–4
Burkeman, Oliver 207–9
'burning platform', problem of 212–13
business
   alchemy, practicing 51–2
   customer and 178, 182–3
   essence of 156–7
   generic resources 60
   idea, testing 99
   model frameworks 102–3
   performance in 85
   reach 63
   steps to using Car Wash framework 46–7
   strategy 4–5, 56, 225
   using bundles to transmuting 40–4
Business Model Canvas 103

by-products 87
   information 66

call centres 179–81
Car Wash paradigm 12, 44–7, 81
Cardinal Health 12, 62
   alchemy at 36–7
   in Car Wash framework 45
   transmutation of value 37–8
caricatures 165
Caterpillar 43
causal ambiguity 57
change
   accelerating 220
   dilemma 33
   releasing 16, 207–26
Checkland, Peter 166
choice architecture 49–50
circular economy 66, 70
client testimonials,
   deconstructing 184–5
Coca-Cola 61, 92
commodities 36–7
communication trainings 14
competitors 4–5, 58–9
context 58
Costco 4
critical/leap of faith
   assumptions 101–3
cross-pollination technique 170
Crummack, Matthew 74
'customer intimacy' programme 22
customer relationship
   management (CRM) system 4, 24

customers
    as being outside the business 178–9
    bringing inside 15, 177–90
    business and 178, 182–3
    call centres and 179–81
    capturing value from 225
    co-creating value with 182
    creating deep conversations 185–7
    deconstructing client testimonials 184–5
    experiences 115–16, 129–30, 155, 181
    focusing on 113–14
    framing relationships 187
    interaction 63
    inviting to speak to their suppliers' staff 183–4
    issues 63
    journey mapping 178
    knowing what works 190
    limiting attitudes to 180
    listening to 112
    making as hero of the story 188–9
    needs 100–1, 110
    reach to 63
    relationships with 176
    Us and Them 179–81, 189–90
    value as perceived by 51

Daimler 2–3
data and information resources 66, 70
day job, demands of 228
'Day Job' excuse 33–4
de-averaging 86
De Becker and Associates 90
delegation and motivation 204–5
denial 213
design, creating aesthetic value through 44
Deutsche Bank 202–3
Digital Media Technology Lab 114
digitalisation 202
Dilts, Robert 231
Disney 14, 109, 110, 113
Dive Bomber syndrome 36
Douglas Wright Restaurants 189–90
Dragons' Den 62
'driving change' phrase 212
Driving Forces 103
Dropbox 43
Dryburgh, Alastair 30

eBay 106
Eco-Touch 131
The 80/20 Principle (Koch) 86
ELIZA (AI computer program) 148–50
engagement 14, 153
Enron 97, 245
ENSEK 66, 70
enterprise resource planning (ERP) system 24
entrepreneurial assets 55
Environmental, Social and Corporate Governance (ESG) 90
epiphenomenal work 221

Index

Everything You Know About Business is Wrong (Dryburgh) 30
experience
 customers 115–16, 129–30, 155, 181
 intuitions and 102
 learning from 96–9

Facebook 66
Faulkner, Paul 6, 7, 135
FedEx 156
feedback 120–1
 defined 121
 questions 122, 123
Feynman, Richard P. 106
Fiske 85
Foch, Ferdinand 210
Ford 63
Ford Focus 39
Ford, Henry 112, 185, 205
Formula 1 3, 84
Fortune 500 mission statement 154
free-floating abstractions 146, 147
Fresh & Easy 96
Frugal Innovation (Radjou and Prabhu) 130
FT.com 29

Gavin De Becker and Associates 90
GE 14, 99, 113, 128, 130
generalisation, inappropriate 208
generic resources 60, 61
Germanotta, Stefani 239–40
Gervais, Ricky 111
'giving control to get control' idea 16, 191–206

delegation and motivation 204–5
'impossible but fun' challenges 200–2
leader's intent 196–7
mission contract 197
'Responsabilisation' programme 195–6
REWARDS format 197–200
self-regulation 205
Somehow Management 16, 192–5
GlaxoSmithKline 110, 114
goal
 defining in plain words 217
 value of achieving 217
GoCo 74, 79
GoCompare 4, 62, 64, 68
Goldenberg, Jacob 85
Goldman, William 94, 98, 115
Google 63, 65, 66, 69, 154
Google's Waymo 1, 2
Grand Change Initiative 214
Group Casino 83
Grove, Andy 236
Gymshark 65, 69

Haber, Justin 28
Haus of Gaga 240
Hemingway, Ernest 42
Henry, Helga 207
Hidden Resource Inventory tool 13, 55
hidden resources 12–13, 54–5, 60, 62–71
 data and information resources 66, 70

exercise 71
finding personal 234–6
inventory 67–70
know-how resources 65, 69
network resources 64–5, 69
relationship resources 62–3, 68
reusable resources 66, 70
ROI from 67
strategic position resources 63–4, 68
types of 62–6
Hilti 43
Hoffman, Reid 239
Honda 157
HP printers 64, 69
Huffington, Arianna 238
Human, All Too Human (Nietzsche) 144
Hunter, Rob 135
hypothesis 98

ideal conditions, waiting for 207–11, 237–8
Ideo 61
IKEA 5, 56, 155
illusions 26–7, 150
implied resources 3, 13, 60–1, 71, 73–4, 75–90
  capabilities and 82–90
  table 80
  value of looking for 80–2
Importance Trap 208
'impossible but fun' challenges, setting 200–2
inanimate saviour solutions 23–4
Inditex 30

Inside the Box (Boyd and Goldenberg) 85
insights, into customer issues 63
installed base 64
intent, leader's 154–5, 196
International Automotive Component Group 63, 68
Internet of Things 43
Intuit 99
The Invention of Lying (film) 111
IO Studios 4
iPhone 5, 98
isolation 117, 118

Jobs, Steve 57, 110, 228
JP Morgan 61
jugaad 130–1

kick-off events 214
know-how resources 65, 69
Koch, Richard 86
Kodak 22
Korolev, Sergei 205, 206
Kroc, Ray 79
Kroger 83

Lady Gaga *see* Germanotta, Stefani
large company 3
leader
  intent 154–5, 196
  unconscious conspiracy against 229
  visionary 233–4
leadership 153
Lean Canvas 103

Index

Lean Startup
  candidate offerings, identifying 100–1
  conducting the experiment 105–6
  critical assumptions, identifying 101–3
  customer needs, understanding 100–1
  economical experiments to testing assumptions 103–5
  learning from 100–7
  loop 101
  making sense of 'failing fast' 106–7
  ranking assumptions 103, 104
The Lean Startup (Ries) 95
learning, from experience 96–9, 219
lecture 146
Lego 15, 54, 60, 65, 69, 182–3
Leith, Jack Martin 182
'less is more' principle 130–2
LinkedIn 239
lip-service buy-in 215
logical levels
  Dilts' 231–4
  example for visionary leader 234
Lotus Cars 3, 54, 65, 69, 80
'lying' 111

MAN Trucks 12, 43, 45–6
management
  consultants, types of 146
  control 16
  jargon 153
  problem with psychology in 208
  see also 'giving control to get control' idea
managers
  as active contributors 206
  and engineers 163–4
  overlooking resources 22–3
  as problem solvers 19, 22
  responsibility of 192–3
  strategies 56
market position 63
market window 66
The Marlboro Man 91
Marriott 14, 109, 113
Marriott, Bill 113
Mars Rover 192, 196, 206
The Matrix (film) 26
McCain Foods 15, 182
McDonald's 79–80, 81
McKinsey 63, 68
Meharabian, Albert 208
Mercedes Benz 2, 65
Michelin 195–6
micromanagement 16
Microsoft 57, 98
mid-sized company 3
Miller, Don 188
Miller, Jonathan 84
Milnthorpe, Harold 207
mindset, shift in 5–6
Minimum Viable Product (MVP) 103–4, 113
Mintzberg, Henry 97, 165
mise en place phrase 40–1

mission contract 197
MIT 85
mock-ups
　building 113
　taking into virtual world 114
Moleskine notebook 42
'moonshot' projects 1, 243
Morieux, Yves 205
Morrisons 83
motivation and delegation 204–5
Mulally, Alan 29, 118
music tour management
　companies 64, 69
Musk, Elon 1, 26, 222, 228

NaHCO$_3$ (sodium bicarbonate),
　applications of 54
nature *vs* purpose 53–5
Netflix 56, 61
network resources 64–5, 69
new ideas, testing 219
new IT system 23–4
Newton, Isaac 35
Nietzsche, Friedrich 142–3, 221
'no talent' battle 135–6
noticing, power of 122–4
Novum Organum Scientiarum,
　Bacon's 93

Oakley, David 29
Ocado 4, 83
OEM (Original Equipment
　Manufacturer) 162–3
Olsen, Ken 96
Only the Paranoid Survive
　(Grove) 236

Open Space events 171–2, 246
opportunities
　growth 5
　identifying new 12
Option Zero 131–2
organisation(s)
　capability for starting with
　　what works 8–11
　checklist to assessing ability
　　to exploit uncovered
　　potential 10–11
　to uncover hidden potential
　　9–10
　getting out ahead of 229
organisational interventions,
　choosing 170–3
organisational memory 20
outputs, focus on 140–1
over-engineering, avoiding 14
Owen, Harrison 246

The Paradox of Choice
　(Schwarz) 50
Patton, George 198
PayPal 106, 239
performance 85, 121, 128, 173,
　212
Personal Digital Assistants
　(PDAs) 106
Pestell, Karl 54
Peters, Tom 197
Picard, Jean-Luc 192
plain words
　defining goal in 217
　techniques 150–3
plans 13, 94, 221

Index

Platypus 28–9
Polaroid 22
Prabhu, Jaideep 130
pre-conditions, for launching initiative 211
Preston, Craig 135
problems, solving 12, 19, 22, 173–4
procrastination 208, 238
Products-as-a Service (PaaS) 42–3
Profit Amplification 12, 48
purpose *vs* nature 53–5

Radjou, Navi 130
Ranjit Das 99–100
Reagan, Ronald 117
real and espoused priorities 141–2
reality bubbles
  stuck in 114–19
  things to breaking out of 118–19
recognition 86
red teams 59
relationship resources 62–3, 68
Renault 66, 70
replication crisis 208
resilience resources, recognising 89–90
resistance, to change 165, 204, 214
resources
  appreciating 55–9
  generic 60, 61

hidden 12–13, 54–5, 60, 62–71, 234–6
  hunt for 59–71
  implied 3, 13, 60–1, 71, 73–4, 75–90
  reconfiguring 219
  three levels of 3, 59–71
  see also specific entries
'Responsabilisation' programme 195–6
return on investment (ROI)
  focus on 138–40
  from hidden resources 11, 67
reusability 76
reusable resources 66
reverse engineering 13, 73–92
REWARDS delegation format 197–200
  to setting 'impossible but fun' challenge 202
Rich Pictures 166–8
Richards, Chet 197
Ries, Eric 95, 99
risks, reducing 7–8
Rockstar Hire 23
Roddick, Anita 228
Rolls Royce 43
Ryman stationers 42

Salesforce 43
Salesradar 4
Samsung Galaxy 5
SaveStack 74–5
saviour solutions 23, 59, 149

Index

scaling technique 88–9, 218, 234–5
Schwarz, Barry 50
Segway 98
self-regulation 205
Senard, Jean-Dominique 195
737 MAX aircraft 179
Shark Tank 62
Shell 61
Shopper Science Lab (SSL) 114
Sieff, Lord 118
Siemens 63
Silicon Valley tech companies 1
Slywotsky, Adrian 55
smaller company 4
Smets, Michael 87
SNAGS list 237
'so what?' question 133
social complexity 56–7
Socially Responsible Investing (SRI) 90
SocialNet 239
Software-as-as-Service (SaaS) 43
Somehow Management 16, 192–5
Southwest Airlines 5, 56
Space X 222
'starting with what works' approach
  ability to 8, 216
  advantage of 240
  based on strengths/resources 22–31
bringing customers inside 15, 177–90
finding few things that make a difference 14, 125–44
fixed purposes, escape from 12–13, 53–71
giving control to get control 16, 191–206
idea of 17
leading to inimitable advantages 57
let the world teach us what works 13, 93–107
making formidable competitor 4–5
making hard to copy 59
organisation's capability for 8–11
paying attention to what actually happens 13–14, 109–24
principles 12–16
recombining existing elements 12, 33–52
reducing risks 7–8
releasing change by 16, 215–19
reverse engineering 13, 73–92
Us and Them stories 15, 159–76
using plain words to describe what you want 14–15, 145–58
Stepford Wives (film) 115

257

Index

Stol, Clifford 97
strategic position resources 63–4, 68
Strategy Maps 103
Sun Tzu 90
sunk cost fallacy 34
survival challenges, handling 89–90
Sutherland, Rory 49, 110
systems and software 65
Szent-Györgyi, Albert 73

Taleb, Nassim 90
talents, ability to attracting 65
tangible/intangible assets 61
targets 143
temptation, resisting 134–5
Tesco 63, 68, 96
Tesla 1, 2, 3
testimonials
  client 184–5
  noticing 86
third-party relationships 64
3M 195
TO DO list 238
TO STOP list 237
Total Person Inventory 161–2, 235–6
tour management companies 64, 69
Toyota Production System 58
trade-offs 58
transformation 14, 153
transmutation 40, 236
troubleshooter documentary technique 151–3

truck manufacturer, in 'Car Wash' options 46

The Unconscious Conspiracy (Bennis) 229
Unipart 80
urgency, emphasising 214
Us and Them
  case study 169–70
  cross-pollination technique 170
  deadly embrace of 162–4
  dynamics, working with 165–75
  Open Space and 171–2
  organisational interventions, choosing 170–3
  problem solving 173–4
  redefining 166
  reframing 174–5
  Rich Pictures 166–8
  stories 15, 159–76
  taking customer relationships beyond 189–90
use *vs* utilise 31
user community 65

vague language and artificial intelligence 146–50
valuable resources
  appreciating 55–8
  exercise 58–9
value 51
  elements, identifying 46, 47
  gap 216–18
Vauxhall Astra 39

Virgin Bank 75
Virgin Upper Class 41
Viscofan 30
Vision Express 156
von Foerster, Heinz 121
Voskhod-1 205
VRIO criteria 56, 61
VUCA 33, 243

Wang, Vera 239
waste, worst kind of 127–8
Webvan 95, 106

WeFlip 74
Weisenbaum, Joseph 148–9
Weiss, Alan 44
Wilk, James 244

Xerox 41

Zanuck, Darryl 97
Zappos 13, 95, 102, 104
Zara 56
Zoom 43, 57, 114

Acknowledgements

Thanks first to Karl Pestell and Debbie Jenkins. They are basically this book's Uncle and Aunt. Their contributions were particularly appreciated during the book's adolescence!

Thanks to Mark Levy, a master of starting with what works, who helped me to recognise what I should be writing about, and then to transform the way I wrote about it.

Thanks to Rory Sutherland for generously writing the Foreword, and for inspiration, enthusiasm and often hilarious conversation.

Thanks to Alan Weiss, whose mentoring has transformed what I believed possible for an independent management advisor.

Many business leaders have helped shape my thinking and contributed examples. I'd especially like to thank Rooney Anand, former CEO of Greene King; Matthew Crummack, CEO of GoCompare; Doug Wright, CEO of Wright Restaurants t/a McDonalds; Paul Faulkner, CEO of Greater Birmingham Chambers of Commerce and former CEO of Aston Villa Football Club; David Pritchett, Former President of Rieke Packaging Systems; Fiona Allan, CEO of The Birmingham Hippodrome and President of UK Theatre; Hanifa Shah, Pro-Vice Chancellor at Birmingham City University; Zoe Whatmore, Chief of Staff at Deutsche Bank and Nancy MacKay, Founder and CEO of MacKay CEO Forums.

Interchange Research founder and Oxford philosopher James Wilk has had a huge influence on the way I think about organisations

Acknowledgements

and successful intervention, as has Interchange's North America President, Dave Franzetta.

Michael Smets of Oxford University's Saïd Business School helped with formative discussions, and Ranjit Das from Strathclyde Business School's Hunter Centre for Entrepreneurship illuminated the nuances of lean startup in an enterprise environment.

Jack Martin Leith and Dian-Marie Hosking helped with many discussions on large group interventions and releasing – rather than driving – change.

Craig Preston, former MD of the Inspirational Development Group, and Tim Baines of Aston Business School helped with case examples.

Thanks to many members of Alan Weiss's consulting community, especially Ann Latham, Amanda Setili, Rick Pay, Lorraine Moore, Val Wright, Colleen Francis, Linda Popky and Mark Donovan, for support, advice and encouragement.

I'd like to give a special mention to Alastair Dryburgh, who is as at home discussing Kierkegaard as Cryptocurrencies, for rigorously challenging my assumptions and always having a point of view I hadn't considered.

Great representation makes a huge difference and I'm extremely grateful to literary agent extraordinaire Kizzy Thompson for all her help. Thanks also to Patrick Nelson of Speakers Associates for introducing us.

Huge thanks to my publisher Eloise Cook for seeing the potential in my original proposal. Eloise provided invaluable help shaping the idea and incisive feedback during the writing process. She and the team at Pearson have been fantastic to work with.

Most importantly, thank you to Barbara for her unwavering support – when authors thank their loved ones for putting up with months of lost weekends, believe me, this is a real thing.

About the Author

Andy Bass is the founder of BassClusker Consulting, an executive advisory firm that helps organisations grow faster by using resources they have already.

He has advised leaders in more than 30 industries, including professional services, finance, technology, manufacturing, health, media, education and the arts.

Andy is also a Forum Chair for MacKay CEO Forums, an international peer-to-peer learning organisation for CEOs and senior executives.

He has taught at Warwick, Strathclyde and Aston Business Schools.

Andy has written three books: *Start With What Works: A Faster Way to Grow Your Business*, *The Performance Papers: Incisive Briefings for Busy Leaders* and *NetworkAbility: Building Your Business One Relationship at a Time* (with Helga Henry).

He has a PhD from Aston University in Computer Science.

About the Author

Publisher's Acknowledgements

6 **Paul Faulkner:** Quoted by Paul Faulkner; **29-30 Financial Times Limited:** FT.com on May 24, 2013 carried an interesting article by David Oakley, Investment Correspondent; **55 Adrian Slywotsky:** Quoted by Adrian Slywotsky; **56 Jay Barney:** Quoted by Jay Barney; **57 Sage Publications:** Barney, Jay (March 1991). "Firm Resources and Sustained Competitive Advantage". Journal of Management. 17 (1): 99–120; **73 Albert Szent-Györgyi:** Quoted by Albert Szent-Györgyi; **74 Matthew Crummack:** Quoted by Matthew Crummack; **90 Nassim Taleb:** Quoted by Nassim Taleb; **90 Sun Tzu:** Sun Tzu, The Art of War; **93 Francis Bacon:** Francis Bacon, (1620), Novum Organum Scientiarum ('New Instrument of the Sciences'); **94 William Goldman:** Quoted by William Goldman; **96 Ken Olsen:** Quoted by Ken Olsen; **97 Darryl Zanuck:** Quoted by Darryl Zanuck; **97 Clifford Stol:** Quoted by Clifford Stol; **97 Steve Ballmer:** Quoted by Steve Ballmer; **97 Harvard Business School:** Mintzberg, Henry (2001) How to overcome change fatigue. Harvard Management Communication Letter, Vol. 4, No. 7, July 2001; **101 and 104 Ranjit Das:** Adapted from Ranjit Das, used with permission; **106 Richard P. Feynman:** Richard P. Feynman, Joint winner of the Nobel Prize in Physics 1965; **112 and 185 Henry Ford:** Quoted by Henry Ford; **121 Heinz von Foerster:** Quoted by Heinz von Foerster; **135 Rob Hunter:** Quoted by Rob Hunter;

Publisher's Acknowledgements

136 Craig Preston: Quoted by Craig Preston; **137 John R. Boyd:** Quoted by John R. Boyd; **142 Friedrich Nietzsche:** Quoted by Friedrich Nietzsche **152 Andrew Bass:** © Andrew Bass 2008; **154 Ashland Inc.:** Mission Statement of Ashland Inc.; **167 Andrew Bass:** Networkability: Building Your Business One Relationship At A Time, by Helga Henry and Andy Bass, reproduced with permission; **190 Douglas Wright:** Quoted by Douglas Wright; **198 George Patton:** Quoted by George Patton; **207 Harold Milnthorpe:** Quoted by Harold Milnthorpe; **209 Gaurdian News & Media Limited:** Oliver Burkeman, Putting off the important things? It's not for the reasons you think, Guardian 19 May 2017; **213 Hilaire Belloc:** Hilaire Belloc; **231 Robert Dilts:** Robert Dilts, Visionary Leadership Skills (1996).